T0128501

AN
INTRODUCTION
TO
SEMANTICS

Dr. Muhammad Ali Alkhuli

| الناشر : دار الفلاح للنشر والتوزيع
ص. ب 818
صويلح 11910
الأردن
هاتف وفاكس 5411547 - 009626 | Publisher: DAR ALFALAH
P. O. Box 818
Swaileh 11910
Jordan
Tel & Fax 009626 - 5411547 |

1

2008 Edition

الناشر : دار الفلاح للنشر والتوزيع ص. ب 818 صويلح 11910 الأردن هاتف وفاكس 5411547 - 009626	*Publisher :* DAR ALFALAH P. O. Box 818 Swaileh 11910 Jordan Tel & Fax 009626 - 5411547

رقم الإيداع لدى دائرة المكتبة الوطنية

2002 / 6 / 1483

420
Alkhuli, Muhammad Ali
An Introduction to Semantics / Muhammad Ali Alkhuli . Amman
: Dar Al Falah, 2002
(184 p.)
Deposit No. : 1483 / 6 / 2002
Descriptors : English Language / Semantics
* تم إعداد بيانات الفهرسة والتصنيف الأولية من قبل دائرة المكتبة الوطنية .

رقم الإجازة المتسلسل لدى دائرة المطبوعات والنشر 1410 / 6 / 2002

ISBN 9957 – 401 – 49 – 1 (ردمك)

بسم الله الرحمن الرحيم

CONTENTS

Preface 8
Chapter 1 . Introduction 9
The Triangle of Meaning 9
Types of meaning 11
Meaning and Information 13
The Semantic Theory 13
Sentence and Utterance 14
Sentence and Proposition 15
Proposition, Sentence, and Utterance 17
Sense and Reference 18
Referring Expressions and Referents 19
Sense and Referent 21
Exercises 21

Chapter 2.   The Concept of Reference 25
Referring expressions 26
The Equative Sentence 27
Predicator 28
Predicate 29
Predicate Degree 30
Reference and Definiteness 32
Referring Expression and Predicate 33
Generic Sentence 33
Universe of Discourse 34
Deictic Words 36
Extension 38
Prototype 39
Exercises 40
Chapter 3.   Similarity of Senses 44

Synonymy 44
Paraphrase 47
Hyponymy 48
Hyponymy-Synonymy Relationship 49
Entailment 50
Entailment-Paraphrase Relationship 52
Entailment-Hyponymy Relationship 53
Exercises 55

Chapter 4. **Dissimilarity of Senses** 62
Antonymy 62
Binary Antonymy 63
Converse Antonymy 65
Gradable Antonymy 66
Perpendicular Antonymy 67
Extensional Antonymy 67
Partial Antonymy 68
Cyclic Antonymy 69
Rank Antonymy 70
Affinity Antonymy 71
Bilateral and Multiple Antonymy 72
Contradictoriness 73
Antonymy-Contradictoriness Relation 75
Exercises 76

Chapter 5. **Ambiguity of Senses** 81
Homonymy 82
Polysemy 83
Homonymy and Synonymy 85
Accounting for Polysemy and Homonymy. 86
Sentence Ambiguity 87
Word-Ambiguity and Sentence Ambiguity. 88
Grammatical Ambiguity 89

Sentence Ambiguity and Paraphrase 90
Exercises 91

Chapter 6.   **The Types of Meaning**   95

Analytical   Meaning   and   Synthetic
   Meaning ……………………………...   95

Contradiction ……………………..   97

Lexical   Meaning   and   Grammatical
   Meaning ……………………………...   98

Meaning and Context …………………   100

Meaning and External Factors ………….   101

Relative Meaning ………………………...   102

Psychological Meaning …………………   103

Literal Meaning and Figurative Meaning ...   104

Meaning and Definition …………………   105

Meaning and Stereotype …………………   106

Basic Meaning and Secondary Meaning …   107

Stylistic Meaning ………………………   108

Echoic Meaning ………………………..   109

Semantic Units …………………………...   109

Meaning and Parts of Speech ……………   110

Meaning and Roles ………………………   111

Exercises ………………………………   113

Chapter 7.   **The Analysis of Meaning**   118

Word Form ……………………………   118

Word Distribution ………………………..   119

Meaning of Meaning ……………………   120

Semantic Features ………………………..   120

Types of Semantic Features ……………..   121

Relations between Semantic Features ……   122

Semantic Features and Synonymy ……….   123

Semantic Features and Antonymy ……….   123

Basic Semantic Features …………………   125

Rules of Semantic Features ……………   126

Measurement of Meaning ………………...   127

Exercises ………………………………   129

Chapter 8.   **Semantic Fields** 133
     Nature of the Semantic Field 133
     Members of the Semantic Field 134
     Multiple Membership 135
     Examples of Semantic Fields 136
     Words and Semantic Fields 137
     Types of Semantic Fields 137
     Relations within the Semantic Field 138
     Applications of Semantic Fields 139
     Exercises 140

Chapter 9.   **Meaning and Logic** 144
     Logical Words 144
     The Logic of *And* 144
     Inference from *And* 145
     Truth Probalilities of *And* 146
     The Logic of *Or* 148
     Truth Probalilities of *Or* 149
     The Logic of *But* 150
     The Logic of Negators 152
     Truth Probabilities of Negators 153
     The Logic of *If* 154
     Exercises 155

Answers to the Exercises 158
Selected Bibliography 169
Appendix I : Symbols 174
Appendix II : Abbreviations 175
Subject Index 176
The Author's Books 182

TABLES

Table (3 – 1) : Relations between some Terms 53

Table (4 – 1) : Quadrilateral Relations 65

Table (4 – 2) : Sense Relations 74

Table (5 – 1) : Homonymy, Polysemy, and Synonymy ... 86

Table (7 – 1) : Antonymy and Semantic Features 124

Table (7 – 2) : Meaning-Measurement Scale 128

Table (9 – 1) : Truth Probabilities of *And* 147

Table (9 – 2) : Truth Probabilities of *Or*.................... 150

Table (9 – 3) : Truth Probabilities of *But* 152

FIGURES

Figure (1 – 1) : The Triangle of Meaning 10

Figure (4 – 1) : Types of Antonymy 73

PREFACE

Semantics is a branch of theoretical linguistics, and it is often an obligatory course taken by students majoring in English or in linguistics . Such students may find some interest in this book, especially when similar books are either not available or too complicated for undergraduates .

This book contains nine chapters, discussing these topics respectively : introduction, referring expressions, similarity of senses, dissimilarity of senses, ambiguity of senses, types of meaning, analysis of meaning, semantic fields, and finally the relation between meaning and logic . Every chapter ends in an adequate number of exercises .

At the end of the book, there are the following : (1) answers to the exercises, (2) selected bibliography, (3) an appendix for symbols, (4) an appendix for abbreviations, and (5) a subject index . Whenever the student finds a new symbol, he is to refer to Appendix I at the end of the book to know the indication of the symbol . For abbreviations, he is to refer to Appendix II .

This book is designed to be a textbook for university students taking a course on semantics . It is hoped that it may be useful as a general reference as well .

Author
Dr. Muhammad Ali Alkhuli

CHAPTER 1

INTRODUCTION

Semantics, as the morphology of the term tells, is the study of meaning, i.e., meanings of words and sentences . Semantics is a branch of linguistics . As we know, linguistics is divided into two major branches : theoretical linguistics and applied linguistics . Theoretical linguistics mainly includes syntax, morphology, phonetics, the history of language (L), and semantics . On the other hand, applied linguistics mainly includes language teaching, L testing, lexicography, translation, psycholinguistics, and sociolinguistics .

The Triangle of Meaning

The word is to be heard or read . Thus, it has two forms : the audible or *spoken form,* which consists of phones that we hear through our ears and the readable or *written form,* which consists of **graphemes,** i.e., letters, that we can perceive through our eyes . The word has a **meaning** stored inside our minds, and it has a **referent** in the world around us . This referent can be a person, animal, or thing .

Therefore, there are three different concepts : word, meaning, and referent . These concepts are different from one another, yet they are strongly related . The first among the three to exist is the referent, of course, because the being precedes the word in existence . The referent exists first, then the word comes accompanied with its meaning that points to the referent .

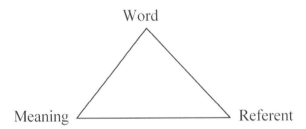

Figure 1 – 1 : The Triangle of Meaning

In semantics, meaning is not related to words only, but to sentences as well . In fact, in actual usage of L for communication, we use sentences more often than isolated words . In both cases, i.e., words and sentences, the main purpose of L is to convey meanings from the speaker to the hearer or from the writer to the reader .

Types of Meaning

Let us assume that an employee has made a serious mistake, which has angered his boss . The boss said, " You've done a great job, man ." The boss, in fact, wanted to blame the employee, but, instead, he praised him . Did the boss really mean what he said ? Certainly, he didn't . He said something and meant something else .

This shows us that there are different types of meaning :

1. **The sentence meaning** (M_1) **.** It is the meaning conveyed by the sentence as it neutrally stands, i.e., as its surface structure tells, without relating it to the speaker's intentions or the speech context .

2. **The speaker's meaning** (M_2). It is the meaning intended by the speaker . This meaning *may* contradict the sentence meaning : the sentence may say something, but the speaker means something else . The speaker's meaning can be revealed through the speaker's facial features, voice tone, eye looks, the general context, or the kind of relationship that exists between the speaker and the hearer . Some or all of these factors combined together help the hearer to determine if the speaker's meaning matches the sentence meaning or not .

3. **The hearer's meaning** (M_3) **.** It is the meaning understood by the addressee or hearer . When you hear a sentence, you may

get angry, and the speaker astonishingly says to you, " Why have you got angry ? I haven't meant what you have understood ." This proves that the hearer may get a meaning different from the speaker's meaning . The speaker may mean *praise,* but the hearer understands *blame* . The speaker may mean *fun,* but the addressee understands *seriousness,* or vice versa . The previous situation is an example of misunderstanding or miscommunication .

Thus, the sentence may have three meanings . The first is the **sentence meaning** as it stands neutrally, independent of any context or situation, dependent on its lexemes and grammatical structure . The second is the **speaker's meaning** as meant by the speaker . The third is the **hearer's meaning** as understood by the hearer .

We may have a variety of relations among the three meanings :

1. The three meanings may be identical : $M_1 = M_2 = M_3$, which is the most common situation .
2. The three meanings are different : $M_1 \neq M_2 \neq M_3$.
3. $M_1 = M_2$, but M_3 is different .
4. $M_1 = M_3$, but M_2 is different .
5. $M_2 = M_3$, but M_1 is different .

Meaning and Information

The sentence, basically, has a meaning, and it is spoken to inform the hearer, especially in a dialogue or conversational situation . But it often happens that we say a sentence not to inform, but to establish or reinforce social relations . For example, when you say to someone, " It is cold today," you are not informing him of what he does not know . Your purpose here is merely to chat, to start a conversation, to initiate a new social relationship, or to reinforce an old one . Most sentences are informative, but not all . Some sentences have **zero information,** and their sole function is social .

The Semantic Theory

Semantics is a general science that deals with all languages, not with one single language . The examples may be in a certain language, but the semantic theory itself applies to all languages .

All that has been said so far in this book applies to all languages . Every L has a triangle of meaning and three types of meaning (M_1, M_2, M_3) . Similarly, all that will be said later in this book applies to all L's .

As the chemical theory is universal, and the physical theory is similarly so, the semantic theory is universal as well, i.e., applicable to all L's . In fact, all scientific facts and theories are universal .

13

Sentence and Utterance

The sentence, a semantic unit, has several definitions . Here, in semantics, a special definition is needed . A **sentence** (S) is an ideal combination of words concatenated horizontally in accordance with special syntactic rules, and it is realized in the spoken or written form .

In contrast, the **utterance** could be one word or more, a whole S or part of it, spoken with a pause before and a pause after . If we have a sentence like *The boy answered all the questions by himself,* this S could be one utterance if spoken with one pause before and one after . The same S could be eight utterances if a pause comes after every word; it could be two utterances or more, depending on how it is spoken .

Therefore, we can see these differences between the S and the utterance (U) :

1. The S is abstract, whereas the U is real speech attached to a certain place, time, speaker, hearer, and situation .

2. The S is a complete syntactic unit, whereas the U may be syntactically complete or not since it may be only a part of the S .

3. The S is turned real through the U .

4. The same S can be turned into one U or more, depending on the number of pauses made during saying the S .

5. The same S can be realized through millions of U's. Whenever the S is spoken, it becomes a new different U since every U has a different situation (speaker, hearer, time, place, occasion) and different phonetic qualities (stress, intonation, articulation).

In this book, from now on, to distinguish the S from the U, the S will be written in *italics,* whereas the U will appear between *quotation marks*. Notice that in daily conversation, people often use parts of sentences and complete sentences as well.

Sentence and Proposition

Before we say a S, there is an idea in the mind, which we will call a **proposition** (P). We first think, then we from a S, and finally we change the S into an U. The P is the essence of meaning. If a statement is used, it asserts the P, e.g., S_1. In contrast, if a question is used, it contains a P asked about, but not asserted, e.g., S_2. If an imperative is made, it also contains the P demanded to be carried out, but not asserted, e.g., S_3.

1. He left for London.
2. Did he leave for London ?
3. Close the door.

The P may be true or false. If the P matches reality, it is true, e.g., *The earth is spherical*. If it does not, it is false, e.g., *The earth is flat*.

15

From now on, in this book, the S will appear in italics, the U between quotation marks, and the P in the normal form of writing .

The truth and falsity of the P entails the truth and falsity of the S and the U . If the P is true, both the S and the U are true . If the P is false, both the S and the U are similarly false .

Thus, the S can be true or false, and can be grammatically correct or incorrect . Look at these sentences :

4. *The earth goes round the sun .*
5. *The sun goes round the earth .*
6. * *The sun go round the earth .*
7. * *The earth go round the sun .*

S_4 is both true and (grammatically) correct . S_5 is false but correct . S_6 is both false and incorrect . S_7 is true but incorrect . This shows that the concepts of *true / false* are here different from those of *correct / incorrect* . The **concept of truth** is dependent on meaning, but the **concept of correctness** is dependent on grammar .

The P is independent of L . If we bring five persons of different native L's, and they observe the same event, they will most probably form the same P's since they have a common universal human tool, i.e., the brain . When it comes to the S and the U, each of them will express the same P in a different S and different U, depending on his native L .

Proposition, Sentence, and Utterance

How are these three concepts of P, S, and U related ? Where are they similar or different ?

1. As for voice loudness, the P and the S have no loudness because they are abstract, but the U has .

2. As for grammatical correctness, the P has no correctness since it is language independent, but the S and the U have since they can be correct or incorrect .

3. As for the information value, all the P, S, and U can be true or false, depending on matching reality .

4. As for dialect, the P has no dialect since it is L independent . The S has no dialect since it is abstract . The U has a dialect, depending on the speaker's dialect .

5. As for L dependence, the P is L independent, but both the S and the U are L dependent .

6. As for abstractness, the P and the S are abstract, but the U is real and actual .

7. As for order, the P exists first, followed by the S, which is realized by an U .

Notice that the same P can be expressed in many S's, and the same S can be realized in millions of U's . For example, the P that Ali broke the window can be expressed in more than ten S's :

17

1. Ali broke the window .

2. The one who broke the window is Ali .

3. Ali is the one who broke the window .

4. The breaker of the window is Ali .

5. Ali is the breaker of the window .

6. He who broke the window is Ali .

7. Ali is he who broke the window .

8. The window was broken by Ali .

9. It is Ali who broke the window .

10. What Ali did was to break the window .

These ten S's belong to the same P, and each of them can be realized by millions of U's, depending on different situations and different speakers .

Sense and Reference

Every academic field has its own terms, and so does semantics . In this field, each of the terms " sense " and " reference " has its own indication . The **sense** of a word explains its relations with other words in the same language, e.g., *rich* is a synonym of *wealthy*, *go* is the opposite of *come*, and *orange* is a kind of *fruit* . In contrast, **reference** is the relation of the word with the external world . It is the relation between the word and the being which it refers to and which exists in the outside world . This being could be a human, animal, plant, thing, or place, e.g., *John, lion, tree, stone, and Rome,* respectively .

There is a difference between words and beings . The word *chair,* for example, is not a chair, nor is the word *car* a car . Words are language expressions, and they are part of L . Beings referred to by words are external entities, and they are part of the external world . Reference is the relation between words and these beings .

We shall call the L expression that refers to an external being a **referring expression** (RE) and call the external being a **referent** (R) . The relation between the RE and the R is reference .

Referring Expressions and Referents

Not all L expressions are referring expressions (RE's), and not all external beings are referents (R's) .In the sentence *The cat looks like the tiger,* we are not referring to a specific cat or tiger, but indicating cats and tigers in general . Thus, *cat* here is not a RE, nor is *tiger* .

Look at this utterance (U) : " Have you seen the cat ? " The *cat* here is a RE because the speaker is asking about a specific cat, which is the referent of this RE .

The RE may be one word or more . For example, " the boy under the tree " is a RE consisting of five words; " Paris " is a RE consisting of one word only . Notice that the same LE may be a RE or not, depending on the situation . *Tree* in " the boy under the tree " is a RE, but *tree* in " The tree may be evergreen or not " is not a RE . The RE must refer to a specific being in the external world .

The referent (R) may be constant or changeable for the same RE . Look at these RE's : " the sun," " the moon," " London," " Makkah," " Jerusalem," " Paris " .If these RE's are repeated millions of times by different people, they always refer to the same R's . These are examples of **constant R's** of the same RE .

Look at these referring expressions (RE's) : " the King   of England," " the President of the USA," and " the Minister of Education ". The referent of each changes from time to time . For instance, the US president now is not the same person before twenty years . These are examples of **changeable R's** of the same RE .

Consider this U : " My left hand ." This RE does not have a constant R . If twenty persons say the same U, each one will be talking about his own left hand . Here is an example where changing the speaker changes the R : one RE, but twenty different R's .

If you say, " I'm going to the capital," *the capital* is a RE, but its R depends on the speaker and on his location, i.e., the country he is in . *The capital* here is a RE with a changeable R .

In some cases, the R is the same although the RE's are different . If you say, " The capital of France," or " Paris," you are indicating the same R although you are using different RE's .

Sense and Referent

There are several differences between the sense and the referent (R) :

1. Sense is the relation between a language expression (LE) and other LE's in the same language (L), but the R is a specific being in the external world .

2. Sense is not related to words only, but to phrases and sentences as well, e.g., *book, in the book, the book is useful,* but the R is related to RE's only . The sentence does not have a R; only the RE has a R .

3. Sense is abstract, but the R is often real and concrete, existing in the external world, e.g., *the sun* .

4. Every meaningful LE has a sense, but not every LE has a referent . For example, in the U " Science is useful," there are no RE's and, consequently, no R's are involved .

EXERCISES

Exercise 1 - 1

Fill in each blank with one suitable word .

1. Semantics is the study of _____ .

2. Semantics is a branch of theoretical _____ .

3. The triangle of meaning includes the word, meaning, and _____ .

4. The word has a _____ form and a _____ form .

5. Meaning exists in the human _____ , but the referent exists in the external _____ .

6. Language is usually used to exchange _____ , but it is sometimes used to develop _____ relations .

7. The utterance may have three meanings : the _____ meaning, _____ meaning, and _____ meaning .

Exercise 1 - 2

Are these statements true (T) or false (F) ?

1. The sentence meaning may contradict the speaker's meaning . _____

2. The speaker's meaning may contradict the hearer's meaning . _____

3. All sentences aim at providing the hearer with new information . _____

4. Every L has a special semantic theory . _____

5. The U is a complete spoken S . _____

6. The S is as real as the U . _____

7. Truth applies to the P only, not to the S or the U . _____

8. The P may be grammatically correct or incorrect . _____

9. The S truth is related to information, but correctness is related to grammar . _____

10. The P is L dependent . ...

11. Sense and reference are synonymous terms . ...

12. The same P can be expressed by different S's in one L or more . ...

Exercise 1 - 3

Give one example of each :

1. a true correct S : _____

2. a false incorrect S : _____

3. a true incorrect S : _____

4. a false correct S : _____

Exercise 1 - 4

Fill in the slots with (+) if the concept is applicable and with (–) if not applicable .

No.	Concept	Proposition	Sentence	Utterance
1.	voice loudness			
2.	grammatical correctness			
3.	informational truth			
4.	showing a dialect			
5.	language dependent			
6.	abstract			

Exercise 1 - 5

Decide whether each is true (T) or false (F) .

1. Sense and reference are synonyms . ...

2. *He went to school .* This is an U . ...

3. *John* is always a RE .   _____

4. *Honest* is a RE .   _____

5. A RE is any E with a sense .   _____

6. The R is the same as reference .   _____

7. The RE is the same as the R .   _____

8. Sense applies to words, phrases, and sentences .   _____

9. The RE has one word only .   _____

10. The same RE may have different R's .   _____

11.Different RE's may have the same R .   _____

Exercise 1 - 6

Which referent is constant (C) and which one is not constant (NC) ?

1. " The capital of Egypt "   _____

2. " Baghdad "   _____

3. " Mars "   _____

4. " His book "   _____

5. " The Mediterranean Sea "   _____

6. " Her father "   _____

CHAPTER 2

THE CONCEPT OF REFERENCE

The concept of reference may require more elaboration . As explained before, reference is the relation between a RE and its R. However, not all language expression (LE's) are RE's . In fact, LE's can be classified into four types :

1. Some LE's are always used as RE's, e.g., *my father, London, Cairo, Amman* . Whenever we use such LE's, they refer to a specific being existent in the external world . Such LE's always have their R's; therefore, they are RE's i.e., **referring expressions** .

2. Some LE's can be RE's or not, depending on the situation which they are used in . In the utterance (U) " Look ! A man is coming," *man* is a RE because it refers to a specific R . In the U " He needs a man to help him," *man* is not a RE; it is a **predicating expression** (PE) .

3. Some LE's cannot have R's at all; they cannot be used as RE's; they are always used as PE's, e.g., *quickly, honest, immediately*.

4. Some LE's cannot be RE's or PE's, e.g., *or, and, on*. They include conjunctions, preposition, negators, and similar particles. Such LE's are called **linking expressions**.

Referring Expressions

Which language expressions (LE's) can be referring expressions (RE's) ? The typical LE's that can be RE's are the following :

1. **The definite NP**, e.g., *the man, this brave man, the man under this tree*. If the NP is definite, it *tends* to be a RE. However, not all definite NP's make RE's; it depends on the situation. In the U " Look at the car," *the car* is a RE, but in the U " The car is faster than the ship," *the car* is not a RE.

2. **The proper noun**, e.g., *London, John, the Red Sea*. This includes the names of persons, countries, cities, rivers, seas, oceans, mountains, etc. Such LE's are usually RE's unless they occur in negative utterances (U's). In the U " He flew to London," *London* is a RE, but in the U " There is no London in Italy," *London* is not a RE simply because it has no R in this case.

.

3. **Personal pronouns**, i.e., pronouns that refer to specific beings, e.g., *I, he, it, they*. Such pronouns are usually RE's, but not always. In the U " If you want to pass, you should study,"

you here may not be a RE because it may mean " any person," not necessarily the addressed person .

The Equative Sentence

We sometimes have two RE's for one R, e.g., *Paris, the capital of France* . These two RE's can make one sentence that is called an equative sentence . Look at these sentences :

1. *Paris is the capital of France .*
2. *Hani is the manager .*
3. *The capital of France is Paris .*
4. *The manager is Hani .*

The best test of an equative sentence is **inversion** . Examining the previous S's, we find that S_3 is an inversion of S_1, and S_4 is an inversion of S_2 . This inversion can be expressed in this formula :

RE_1 is $RE_2 \Rightarrow RE_2$ is RE_1 . Such inversion proves that a certain S is equative . Look at these S's :

5. *The city is large .*
6. *The boy is honest .*

The last two S's are not equative because inversion is not possible since S's 7 and 8 are ungrammatical :

7. * *Large is the city .*
8. * *Honest is the boy .*

However, inversion is not the only criterion . Look at this S :

9. *What is needed is a glass of water* .

Here, in S9, inversion is possible : *A glass of water is what is needed* . Nevertheless, S9 is not an equative sentence because it does not have any RE . The equative sentence must meet two criteria . First, it must have two RE's indicating the same R . Second, the sentence must allow inversion .

Predicator

Look at these sentences :

1. *Cairo is a (city) in Africa* .
2. *Ibn Khadun was a (genius)* .
3. *The professor (authored) this book* .

The underlined units in these three S's are RE's because they indicate specific R's . After excluding the RE's from each sentence (S), we look for the most important word in what remains . Such a word is called a **predicator** .

The predicators in these three S's (1-3) are bracketed, and they are *city, genius,* and *authored,* respectively . Notice that the predicator in semantics is different from the predicator in syntax, which is used for the function of the verb .

Examine these sentences :

4. *The book is (on) the shelf* .
5. *The book is (useful)* .
6. *The book was (lost) yesterday* .

28

In sentences (4-6), what is underlined is a RE, and what is bracketed is a predicator . Notice that the predicator can be a preposition (S4), an adjective (S5), a verb (S6), or a noun (S1) .

We must emphasize some points here :

1. Every simple sentence has one predicator only, e.g., S's (1-6) .

2. Every simple sentence may have one RE, e.g., S2, S5, S6, or more, e.g., S1, S3, S4 .

3. Analyzing the S into a *RE and predicator* is completely different from analyzing it into a *subject and predicate* . The first analysis belongs to semantics, whereas the second one belongs to syntax .

Predicate

The *predicator* is a term related to a certain S; it is sentence dependent . In contrast, a **predicate** is any word that may potentially be a predicator . For example, the words *brave, walk, man, boy,* and *on* can be predicators in some sentences, so they are predicates as well . The main difference between the two terms is that the predicator is a word actually used in a certain sentence, whereas the predicate is a word that can be potentially used in a sentence .

The predicate is not necessarily one word although it is usually so; it is sometimes a group of words such as *look into,*

29

look for, switch on, and other prepositional verbs and phrasal verbs .

In a certain S or U, the predicator has one meaning only in the writer's or speaker's mind . Talking about several meanings of the predicate is merely an analytical outlook .

The simple S has one predicator only, but it may include several predicates . In the U " Look at this beautiful bird with its beautiful colors," the predicator is *look at,* but *beautiful* is a predicate here, which can be a predicator in other possible sentences .

Predicate Degree

In one simple sentence, there may be one RE or more, with one predicator . However, different predicators require a different number of RE's in the same S . Look at these S's :

1. *The boy (slept) .*
2. *He (ate) the apple .*
3. *He (gave) his brother a gift .*
4. *Syria is (between) Jordan and Turkey .*
5. *The pen is (under) the book .*
6. *The garden is (beautiful) .*
7. *He is still (a child) .*
8. *John is (a brother) of Robert .*

30

In S's (1-8), the RE is underlined, and the predicator is bracketed . Each predicator needs a certain number of RE's, and this number is called the **predicate degree** . Of course, whatever applies to the predicator applies to the predicate as well .

Analazing S's (1-8), one can see that *slept* needs one RE, so it is a **one-degree predicator** . The predicator *ate* in (S2) is a **two-degree predicator** . The word *gave* (S3) is a **three-degree predicator,** *between* (S4) is three degrees, *under* (S5) is two degrees, *beautiful* (S6) is one degree, *child* (S7) is one degree, and *brother* (S8) is two degrees .

Sentences (1-8) may show us the following :

1. Adjectives are usually one-degree predicates (S6) .

2. Nouns are usually one-degree predicates (S7), but some nouns like *brother, sister,* and *father* are two-degree predicates because each needs two RE's (S8) .

3. The predicator (or predicate) can be a verb (S1, S2, S3), a preposition (S4, S5), an adjective (S6), or a noun (S7, S8).

4. A verb may be one degree (S1), two degrees (S2), or three degrees (S3) .

5. A preposition may be two degrees (S5) or three degrees (S4) .

6. When sentences are made, one must observe the predicate degree; otherwise, the S will not be acceptable .

31

Reference and Definiteness

What is the relation between the RE and definiteness ? Is definiteness a condition of the RE ? Does indefiniteness indicate that the LE is not a RE ? Let us examine these four U's :

1. "The boy is honest ."
2. " The boy may get sick as the girl ."
3. " Look there ! I see a boy climbing the tree ."
4. " A boy must have broken the window ."

In U1, the speaker has a certain boy in his mind; therefore, *the boy* here is a RE . In U2, the speaker talks about boys and girls in general; thus, *the boy* in U2 is not a RE . This proves that the **definite article** *the* is not a condition for the RE . The noun may have *the* before it, yet it is not a RE, e.g., *the boy* in U2 .

In U3, *boy* is a RE although it has an indefinite article before it, because it indicates a specific boy . In contrast, *boy* in U4 is not a RE because it does not indicate a specific boy . This proves that the **indefinite article** does not always negate reference : an indefinite noun (grammatically speaking) can be a RE (U3) or a non-referring expression (U4) .

These four utterances (1-4) show that a definite LE may be a RE or not, depending on the situation . They also show that an indifinte LE may be a RE or not . This means that **definiteness** is a grammatical concept that does not necessarily guarantee **specificity** . The LE may be definite, yet it is not a RE; on the other hand, it may be indefinite, yet it is a RE . " Definite " and " indefinite " are *grammatical terms* not directly parallel to the *semantic terms* " referring expression " (RE) and " non-referring expression " (NRE) .

Referring Expression and Predicate

Can the predicate be a part of a RE ? Look at these sentences :

1. *The (blue) car has arrived .*
2. *Look at the (pretty) cat (at) the (far) corner .*

In (1), *the blue car* is a RE, and *blue* is a predicate, used as part of the RE to help the hearer identify the R . Similarly, in (2), all the underlined phrase is one RE, which includes three predicates between brackets : *pretty* and *at* to help identify the cat and *far* to help identify the corner .

This demonstrates that the RE may include one predicate or more to help the hearer identify the referent .

Generic Sentence

Does every S include a RE ? The answer is No. Some sentences do not indicate specific R's and thus do not have RE's . Look at these sentences :

1. *The believer is kind to people .*
2. *A cow is a mammal .*

3. The plane is faster than the car .

4. Cats look like tigers .

5. Water is essential to life .

6. This cow is sick .

Examining the previous S's, one notices that S's (1-5) indicate *the believer, cow, plane, cats,* and *water* in general; hence, none of them has a RE . Such S's are called **generic sentences** . In contrast, S6 has a RE, i.e., *this cow*, which indicates that S6 is not a generic S .

The **generic noun** in a generic S, in English, can be expressed in different ways :

a. The article *the* before the singular countable noun, as in (1) .

b. The article *a* before the singular countable noun, as in (2).

c. The countable plural noun without an article, as in (4) .

d. The mass noun without an article, as in (5) .

In brief, generic sentences do not have RE's and do not indicate R's .

Universe of Discourse

What is the context of conversation ? It could be real or imaginary . Most artistic works deal with imaginary universes; this is quite obvious in poetry, dramas, novels, short stories, and cartoons, all of which have tragic or comic characters, real or imaginary .

No long discourse can continue without R's and RE's even if these R's are imaginary . **Imaginary referents** do exist in the **imaginary universe;** you may say that such imaginary R's are real in their own world of imagination .

It is mention-worthy that no matter how imaginary the universe is, it cannot be completely so, because the speaker or writer cannot make an absolutely imaginary character or universe owing to his inability to completely rid himself of the real world . In addition, it will be very difficult or rather impossible for the hearer to understand an absolutely imaginary world . The **imaginary world** is never absolutely so : it is always a mixture of reality and imagination . Thus, neither the speaker nor the hearer can escape the effect of the *world of facts* on the *world of fiction* .

If two conversers want to communicate, they must unify their universe of discourse . They both must know whether they indicate the real world or an imaginary world; otherwise, communication would certainly fail .

The topic of discourse usually centers around the RE's, which may indicate real R's or imaginary R's . In chapter 1, it was mentioned that the R must be a specific being in the external world . Here and now, we need to modify this a little by saying that the R need not be real and concrete . In our daily discourse, we treat many LE's as if they are RE's although they do not refer to concrete beings, such as *today, tomorrow, yesterday, next year, 9 o'clock,* etc . Any LE indicating a certain distance, number, or time is a RE, e.g., *ten miles, three hundred, 10 o'clock,* respectively .

Deictic Words

Most L words mean what they mean independent of the situation of usage . In other words, they are not dependent on the speaker, hearer, time, or place of the utterance (U), e.g., *door, chair, car, fan, ship* .

In contrast, every L has some words whose meanings partly depend on the situation . Such words are called **deictic words** (DW), e.g., " you." whose R changes according to the situation . This " you " is one RE, but it has millions of different R's .

Some DW's depend on the speaker, e.g., *I, we* . The R of each depends on who is speaking . Some DW's depend on the place of conversation, e.g., *here, there,* whose R depends on where they are said . The other DW's that depend on place are demonstratives, i.e., *this, that, these, those* . If you say " this city," the R depends on where you are .

Other DW's depend on the time of speaking, e.g., *today, yesterday, tomorrow, tonight, now, last night* . Each of these indicates a different R depending on the time of speaking . For example, *today* can be any day in history, depending on when it was said .

The previously-mentioned DW's are pronouns, demonstratives, some adverbs of time, and some adverbs of place. In addition, there are two DW's that are verbs : *come* and *go* . Their meaning depends on the place of the speaker in relation to the hearer or doer . If the hearer is to move towards the speaker, " *come* " is used . Otherwise, we use " *go* " . If the speaker says, " Come to the school," this means that he himself is at the school . Otherwise, he would say, " Go to the school ."

This explains why we have to change these DW's when we change **direct speech** into reported speech; there is a complete change in situation : a change in the speaker, hearer, time, and place . In most cases, these changes happen : come → *go, I* → *he, we* → *they, here* → *there, now* → *then, this* → *that, yesterday* → *the day before,* for example . Not only this, but tenses also change to suit the new time, e.g., *write* → *wrote, wrote* → *had written* .

Which DW's are to be changed when we change direct speech into **reported speech** depends on whether or not the speaker, hearer, time, or place has changed . If the time has not changed, DW's of time do not change . If the place has not changed, DW's of place do not change, and so on .

Extension

What does a predicate cover ? The predicate *car* covers all cars that may be indicated by this predicate in all places and all times, i.e., the past, present, and future . Such coverage is called the **extension of the predicate** .

Extension differs from sense in two ways . First, extension refers to a group of concrete beings, whereas sense does not . Second, extension connects the predicate with the external world, whereas sense connects the predicate with other words inside the same L . On the other hand, both extension and sense are similar in that they are not dependent on an occasion, situation, or utterance .

Extension, in addition, differs from reference in two ways . First, extension is a group, whereas reference is just a relation between the RE and its R . Second, extension is not dependent on an occasion, situation, or utterance, whereas reference is . On the other hand, both extension and reference are similar in that they connect LE's with the external world .

Of course, it is obvious that *word, sense, extension, reference,* and *referent* (R) are five related terms, yet they are not synonymous . Every word has a sense, but not necessarily an extension; for example, *in* has a sense, but has no extension, no reference, and no R . The R is a member in the extension . Every reference has a R . These five terms are closely related, but each is different from the other four .

Extension is not restricted to nouns only, such as *car, ship, house* . Adjectives such as *red* have extension as well . Anything *red* in all times and places makes the extension of *red* . The predicate extension is all the **potential referents** of that predicate, regardless of time and place .

However, the extension of a predicate is not always clear . We are sometimes not sure whether a thing comes under a certain extension or not . For example, some may raise questions whether the first can come under the extension of the second in these pairs : *boat / ship, bush / tree, lorry / car, hill / mountain, stream / river, lake / sea* .

Prototype

Why are we in doubt whether *bush* comes under the extension of *tree* ? It is because we do not know the accurate qualities or features of *tree* or *bush* . What makes a tree a tree and a bush a bush ? Do the features of *tree* allow *bush* in the membership of *tree* ?

Here comes the **prototype,** which is a typical member in the extension of a certain predicate . The *seal,* for instance, is a *fish,*

39

but not a typical one, i.e., not a prototype, because most fishes do not look like a seal . The *ostrich* is a bird with wings, but not a prototype of *birds* . The *palm-tree* is certainly a *tree*, but not a prototype of trees, because most trees do not look like a palm-tree . Both the *giant* and the *dwarf* are men, but neither is a prototype of *man*, because most men are neither giants nor dwarfs .

Therefore, there are clear differences between the referent (R), extension, and prototype . The R is a being indicated by a RE in a certain utterance in a certain situation . The extension is all potential R's, independent of situations . The prototype is a **typical member** in the extension . For example, the R of " the tree " is a certain tree in a certain situation and certain utterance, and the extension of *tree* is all the trees in all places and all times, whereas the prototype of *tree* is a typical normal tree which is a member in the extension of *tree* .

EXERCISES

Exercise 2 - 1

Which kind of expression is each : always a RE, always a PE, both, or linking expression ?

| 1. Rome | _____ | 5. green | _____ |
| 2. Shakespeare | _____ | 6. if | _____ |

3. honestly   _____   7. doctor   _____

4. accurately   _____   8. and   _____

Exercise 2 - 2

Underline the only predicator in each S :

1. *The capital lies on the sea-shore .*

2. *The man ate the food .*

3. *His car is red .*

4. *He is in Canada .*

Exercise 2 - 3

Underline the RE's in these U's :

1. " He is a skilled doctor ."

2. " Khalid is a brilliant leader ."

3. " You are better than Ali in swimming ."

4. " Planes are similar to birds ."

Exercise 2 - 4

Go back to the previous exercise, and identify the predicates in those utterances .

1. _____

2. _____

3. _____

4. _____

Exercise 2 - 5

Are these sentences equative ?

1. *The chairman is John .*   _____

2. The fastest runner is Ali .   _____

3. Edward is at home .   _____

4. The physician has not come yet .   _____

Exercise 2 - 6

What is the degree of each bold-type predicate ?

*1. The teacher **asked** his student two questions .*   _____

*2. The bird has **flown** away .*   _____

*3. The story is very **interesting** .*   _____

*4. He is John's **father** .*   _____

*5. The ball is **on** the tree .*   _____

Exercise 2 - 7

Is the bold-type LE a RE or a predicate ?

*1. How beautiful **this garden** is !*   _____

*2. His **beautiful** garden needs more attention .*   _____

*3. **Water** is essential to life .*   _____

*4. He works as an **engineer** .*   _____

*5. Adnan is an honest **man** .*   _____

Exercise 2 - 8

Are these sentences generic (G) or non-generic (NG) ?

1. The monkey is a mammal .   _____

2. This bird is very beautiful .   _____

3. Beings are either living or non-living .   _____

4. He bought the house in the suburb .   _____

5. Plants differ from animals .   _____

Exercise 2 - 9

Underline the deictic words in these U's .

1. " I agree with you concerning this issue ."
2. " We will meet here ."
3. " He is not there now ."
4. " Go to him today or tomorrow ."

Exercise 2 - 10

Decide whether each is true (T) or false (F) .

1. Extension is similar to sense in that they both connect the word with the external world . _____
2. Both extension and reference connect the word with the external world . _____
3. The sense and reference of the word are synonyms . _____
4. The reference and referent of a word are synonymous . _____
5. Knowing sense helps to identify extension . _____
6. Extension applies to nouns, but not to adjectives . _____
7. A referent is dependent on a situation . _____
8. The prototype is dependent on a situation . _____
9. The prototype is one of the members of the extension . _____
10. Extension is independent of a situation . _____

CHAPTER 3

SIMILARITY OF SENSES

There are various kinds of relationships between word senses . Such senses may be identical, similar, or different . The same fact is true about sentence senses . In this chapter, we shall see how senses can be identical or similar . In the following chapter, we shall discuss how senses can be different or dissimilar .

Synonymy

Synonymy is the identity of the senses of two words or more . Each word is called a **synonym,** and it is synonymous with the other one or ones .

The best test of synonymy is **replacement** . If a word can replace another without changing the sentence meaning, the two words are synonyms . In the S, *He is a courageous soldier,* we can replace *courageous* with *brave* without affecting the sentence meaning (SM) . As a result, the two words *courageous* and *brave* are synonyms . If we want to use symbols, the relationship can be symbolized like this : *courageous = brave* .

Synonymy, in addition, is mutual . In other words, if word A is synonymous with word B, it follows that word B is synonymous with word A, of course . Synonymy can also be between more than two words, e.g., *bright, clever, intelligent, keen, smart* .

However, synonymy is rarely complete . It is rare to have two **synonymous words** that can replace each other in all contexts . In most cases, synonymy is partial : a word is synonymous with another in some contexts, but not in all . For example, we can say *deep thinking, deep rivers,* and *profound thinking,* but we cannot say *profound rivers .

In fact, some semanticists argue that language cannot possibly have **complete synonyms** . They hold that L does not need two words that are exactly the same in all aspects and all contexts; there must be some difference, no matter how slight it may be, between the two synonyms . Such linguists believe that all cases of synonymy are, in fact, partial, not complete . However, some other semanticists disagree to this view .

It is important to notice that synonymy is dependent on the **basic meaning** of the words, regardless of the secondary, psychological, or stylistic meanings . If the basic meanings of the two words are identical, the two words are synonyms, e.g., *father, male parent* . The psychological meanings of these two words are different, with more emotion attached to the first word, yet the two are synonyms because the basic meanings are the same .

Synonymy is essentially that of senses, not of words . We have to say that the senses of these words are synonyms, because synonymy is mainly a relationship between senses, not between words . Despite this, out of simplicity and brevity, it is acceptable to say that these words are synonyms .

As for synonymy criteria, there are two criteria . The first criterion is **contextual replacement** : one word can replace the other in certain contexts . For example, *He is a teacher of physics,* where *instructor* can replace *teacher,* without changing the SM . This test proves that *teacher* and *instructor* are synonyms . The second criterion is **mutual inclusion** : a *teacher* is a kind of *instructor,* and an *instructor* is a kind of *teacher* . If each word is a kind of the other, the two words are synonyms . Notice that *apple* and *fruit* are not synonyms, because *apple* is a kind of *fruit,* but *fruit* is not a kind of *apple* .

As for grammatical categories, it is common that the two synonyms belong to the same **part of speech** . The two synonyms are frequently verbs, nouns, adjectives, etc. e.g., *clever / bright, cleverly / brightly, cleverness / brightness* . In other words, if the word is a verb, its synonym is usually a verb; if the word is a noun, its synonym is usually a noun too, and so

46

on . However, synonyms may belong to different parts of speech as well, e.g., *cleverness / to be bright* .

Paraphrase

Synonymy is a relationship between words or senses of words, not senses of sentences . However, if two S's are identical in sense, they are called paraphrases, and each one is a paraphrase of the other, e.g., *This is a bent wire & This is a twisted wire* .

This paraphrasing or **paraphrase relationship** can be achieved through two ways . First, we may have two S's identical in all words except two synonyms in the same position, e.g., *He did his homework very quickly & He did his homework very speedily* . In other words, we can make paraphrases through using synonyms . Second, we may make paraphrases through transformation .

To illustrate the second point, look at these sentences :
1. Ali is Hani's father .
2. Hani is Ali's son .
3. The boy broke the window .
4. The window was broken by the boy .
5. The boy was the one who broke the window .
6. John is the manager .
7. The manager is John .

If we examine the previous seven S's, we find that S_1 and S_2 are paraphrases, having the same sense . We also find that S_3, S_4, and S_5 are paraphrases . Similarly, S_6 and S_7 are paraphrases . These paraphrases are not made by using synonyms, but by transforming the grammatical structure of the S into another structure that keeps the sense unchanged. i .e., a change in the structure without a change in sense .

We may express the paraphrase relationship between the previous sentences by using the symbol $\equiv$ to indicate paraphrasing : $S_1 \equiv S_2$, $S_3 \equiv S_4 \equiv S_5$, $S_6 \equiv S_7$.

Paraphrases are always equally true or false . If A and B are paraphrases and A is true. B must be also true . If A and B are paraphrases and A is false. B must be false too . In other words, if A and B are paraphrases, both must be either true or false; it cannot be that one is true and the other is false .

Hyponymy
Look at these pairs of words :

1. lion, animal

2. orange, fruit

3. brother, relative

4. honesty, virtue

The first word in each pair is a kind of the second word . The *lion* is a kind of *animal*, an *orange* is a kind of *fruit*, a *brother* is a kind of *relative*, and *honesty is* a kind of *virtue* .

In other words, *lion* is a **hyponym** of *animal,* and *animal* is a **superordinate** of *lion* . Such a sense relationship is called hyponymy . This **hyponymy** requires two words (or phrases), one of which is a hyponym and the other is a superordinate .

To symbolize such a relationship, we may use the symbol ɔ, which means *a hyponym of :*

lion ɔ animal   *orange ɔ fruit*

brother ɔ relative   *honesty ɔ virtue*

Hyponymy works in one direction only : if A is a hyponym of B, B is not a hyponym of A . Going back to the four examples, the *lion* is a kind of *animals,* but the *animal* is not a kind of *lions* . In other words, every *lion* is an *animal,* but it is not the case that every *animal* is a *lion* .

If A ɔ B, all A's are B's, and some B's are A's, but not all B's are A's . If a *lion* is a hyponym of *animal,* all lions are animals, and some animals are lions, but not all animals are lions .

Hyponymy-Synonymy Relationship

Let us consider synonymy again in light of hyponymy . What is the relationship between synonymy and hyponymy ? If A ɔ B and B ɔ A, A = B . What does this mean ? If A is a hyponym of B and B is a hyponym of A, A and B are synonyms . For example,

49

return ⊃ go back

go back ⊃ return

∴ *return = go back*

Another example is *clever* and *bright* . *Clever* is a hyponym of *bright,* and *bright* is a hyponym of *clever* . In other words, *clever* is a kind of *bright,* and *bright* is a kind of *clever* . Therefore, they are **mutual hyponyms** . Being so, they are synonyms . Symbolically, it is this way :

clever ⊃ bright

bright ⊃ clever

∴ *clever = bright*

This means that synonymy is **mutual hyponymy** .

Entailment

Look at these sentences (S's) :

1. *She saw a boy .*
2. *She saw a person .*
3. *He killed a lion .*
4. *He killed an animal .*

S_1 entails S_2 : if she saw a boy, this necessarily means that she saw a person, because *boy* is a hyponym of *person* . Thus, S_1 entails S_2, and the relationship between S_1 and S_2 is a **relationship of entailment** .

The same relationship applies to S_3 and S_4. S_3 entails S_4, and the two S's are in an **entailment relationship,** because *lion* is a hyponym of *animal* . Notice that entailment is a sense relationship between sentences, not between words .

Entailment requires that if A entails B, the truth of A entails the truth of B . For example, *if he saw a lion, he necessarily saw an animal* . Notice that the truth of B does not necessarily entail the truth of A : *if he saw an animal, this does not necessarily entail that he saw a lion* . Entailment works in one direction only . In addition, entailment does not mean that if A is false, B is false . For example, *if he did not see a lion, this does not mean that he did not see an animal* .

If A entails B, the truth of A necessarily and inevitably entails the truth of B . However, the falsity of A does not entail the falsity of B . In addition, if A entails B, B does not entail A .

Using the symbol $\rightarrow$ to mean *entail,* we can express the previous relationships as follows : $S_1 \rightarrow S_2$, $S_3 \rightarrow S_4$.

Entailment can also be cumulative . If A entails B, and if B entails C, then A entails C . Such entailment can be called **cumulative entailment** . Look at these S's :

5. *The boys saw a lion* .

6. *The boys saw an animal* .

7. *The persons saw an animal* .

51

S_5 entails S_6, and S_6 entails S_7 . Therefore, S_5 entails S_7 . Symbolically, it may expressed as this :

$S_5 \rightarrow S_6$

$S_6 \rightarrow S_7$

$\therefore S_5 \rightarrow S_7$

Entailment-Paraphrase Relationship

Look at these sentences :

1. *The battle ended in a sad way .*

2. *The battle ended in a melancholy way .*

S_1 entails S_2, and S_2 entails S_1 . Therefore, S_1 and S_2 are paraphrases . This means that a paraphrase is a **mutual entailment** . Notice that both paraphrase and entailment are sense relationships between sentences, not between words . The relation between S_1 and S_2 can be expressed symbolically this way :

$S_1 \rightarrow S_2$

$S_2 \rightarrow S_1$

$\therefore S_1 \equiv S_2$

Now remember that we have four different symbols : = for synonymy, $\equiv$ for paraphrases, $\supset$ for hyponymy, and $\rightarrow$ for entailment .

Up till now, we have four different terms : *synonymy, paraphrase, hyponymy,* and *entailment* . The relation between these terms is clearly shown in Table 3 – 1 .

Table 3 – 1 : Relations between some Terms

Relation	Synonymy	Paraphrase	Hyponymy	Entailment
between words	+	—	+	—
between sentences	—	+	—	+
sense identity	+	+	—	—
sense oppositeness	—	—	—	—
in one direction	—	—	+	+
mutual relation	+	+	—	—

Entailment-Hyponymy Relationship

The previous sections have shown that there is a relation between synonymy and paraphrase, a relation between synonymy and hyponymy, and a relation between entailment and paraphrase . Here, in this section, we will discuss the relationship between entailment and hyponymy .

If two sentences A and B are identical in all words except two words C and D in the same position (C in A and D in B) and C is a hyponym of D, it follows that A entails B . This is the basic rule that regulates the relationship between entailment and hyponymy .

Look at these two S's
1. *The farmer was collecting some <u>sheep</u>.*
2. *The farmer was collecting some <u>animals</u> .*

53

S_1 and S_2 are identical in all words except *sheep* in S_1 and *animals* in S_2 in the same position, i.e., finally here in this case. The word *sheep* is a hyponym of *animals*. Therefore, S_1 entails S_2.

However, this basic rule has three exceptions :

1. **Negative sentences**. If S_1 and S_2 are negative and identical in all words except two words in the same position (C in S_1 and D and S_2), and C is a hyponym of D, it follows that S_2 entails S_1. These two S's are an example of the first exception :

   3. The farmer was <u>not</u> collecting some sheep.

   4. The farmer was <u>not</u> collecting some animals.

2. ***All* sentences**. Another exception to the basic rule is *all* S's, i.e., S's that include the word *all*. Look at these two S's :

   5. The farmer was collecting <u>all</u> the sheep.

   6. The farmer was collecting <u>all</u> the animals.

In this case, S_6 entails S_5. In other words, the sentence which has the superordinate entails the sentence which has the hyponym. Without *all*, the basic rule applies, and S_5 entails S_6. With *all*, the basic rule cannot apply, and S_6 entails S_5.

3. **Sentences with relative words**. Another exception to the basic rule is S's which have relative words in the same position, e.g., *large, small, far, near*. Look at these two S's :

54

7. He saw a <u>large</u> mouse .

8. He saw a <u>large</u> animal .

In S_7 there is a hyponym *(mouse)*, and in S_8 there is the superordinate *(animal)* . If he saw a large mouse, this cannot entail that he saw a large animal, because *large* is a relative word with a flexible changeable sense . A funny example is that *a very large mouse is very much smaller than a very small elephant* . In the case of relative words, neither does S_6 entail S_7, nor does S_7 entail S_6 .

To summarize, the basic rule organizes the relationship between entailment and hyponymy, but there are three exceptions . In the basic rule, S_1 has the hyponym and S_2 has the superordinate . The basic rule and the three exceptions give us these four cases :

1. The basic rule : $S_1 \rightarrow S_2$.
2. The negation exception : $S_2 \rightarrow S_1$.
3. The *all* exception : $S_2 \rightarrow S_1$.
4. The relative-word exception : no entailment .

EXERCISES

Exercise 3 - 1

Are these statements true (T) or false (F) ?

1. Most cases of synonymy are complete .   _____

2. Synonymy is basically between words, not between senses .   _____

3. Synonymy depends on the basic sense, not on additional and psychological senses .   _____

4. Some semanticists deny the existence of complete synonymy, which they consider a linguistic waste .   _____

5. Synonymy is a relationship between words and also between sentences .   _____

6. The two synonyms must belong to the same part of speech .   _____

7. Hyponymy is mutual synonymy .   _____

8. Synonymy is mutual hyponymy .   _____

9. Both paraphrase and synonymy are identity of senses .   _____

10. Paraphrases are either both true or both false .   _____

Exercise 3 - 2

Give a synonym of each word .

1. help	_____	5. apex	_____
2. depressed	_____	6. dorsum	_____
3. melancholy	_____	7. affirmative	_____
4. glad	_____	8. instruct	_____

Exercise 3 - 3

Are these pairs of S's paraphrases (P) or not (NP) ?

1. *Town A lies east of town B .*

   Town B lies west of town A . _____

2. *Point A is above point B .*

   Point B is below point A . _____

3. *Village A is after village B .*

   Village B is before village A . _____

4. *Ali is Sameer's son .*

   Jihad is Sameer's son . _____

5. *He offered them a great help .*

   He offered them a great aid . _____

Exercise 3 - 4

How has paraphrasing been achieved in the pairs of Exercise 3 – 3 : through synonymy (S) or through transformation (T) ?

1. Pair 1 in Exercise 3 – 3 : _____

2. Pair 2 in Exercise 3 – 3 : _____

3. Pair 3 in Exercise 3 – 3 : _____

4. Pair 5 in Exercise 3 – 3 : _____

Exercise 3 - 5

What is the symbol of each relationship ?

1. synonymy _____

2. paraphrase _____

3. hyponymy   ....

4. entailment   _____

Exercise 3 - 6

Is each statement true (T) or false (F) ?

1. *fruit* is a hyponym of *apple* .   ...

2. *Plant* is a hyponym of *tree* .   ...

3. Hyponymy has some kind of sense similarity .   ...

4. Hyponymy and synonymy are relations between words, not between S's .   ...

5. Paraphrase and entailment are relations between S's, not between words .   ...

6. *Uncle* is a hyponym of *relative* .   ...

7. Hyponymy is a one-way relationship .   ...

8. Synonymy and paraphrase are one-way relationships .   ...

9. Entailment is a two-way relationship .   ...

10. Entailment indicates sense similarity more than paraphrasing does .   ...

11. Synonymy is sense identity, but hyponymy is sense similarity .   ...

12. *Animal* is the superordinate of *cat* .   ...

13. The superodinate is wider than the hyponym .   ...

14. The hyponym is one kind of the superordinate .   ...

Exercice 3 - 7

What is the relationship between the words of each pair : synonymy (S), hyponymy (H), or superordination (Su) ?

1. cucumber, plant   _____

2. human, child   _____

3. flower, tulip   _____

4. tiger, animal   _____

5. development, growth   _____

6. approach, come close to   _____

7. bravery, courage   _____

Exercice 3 - 8

Are these S's of each pair in a relationship of paraphrase (P) or entailment (E) ?

1. *He got ready for the exam .*

   He got ready for the test .   _____

2. *He grew a lot of trees .*

   He grew a lot of plants .   _____

3. *John is Dick's brother .*

   Dick is John's brother .   _____

4. *Mary is Nancy's mother .*

   Nancy is Mary's daughter .   _____

5. *Ali looks like his father .*

   Ali resembles his father .   _____

6. *He drew a rectangle .*

   He drew a geometrical figure .   _____

59

Exercise 3 - 9

Which sentence entails the other : the first (F) or the second (S) ?

1. *The student bought three books .*

   The student bought three printed materials . _____

2. *The student did not buy any books .*

   The student did not buy any printed materials . _____

3. *The student bought all the books .*

   The student bought all the printed materials . _____

Exercise 3 - 10

Fill in each blank with one suitable word .

1. Both synonymy and _____ are relationships of sense identity .

2. Synonymy is a sense identity of _____ .

3. Paraphrase is a sense identity of _____ .

4. Synonymy is _____ hyponymy .

5. Paraphrase is mutual _____ .

6. Both synonymy and _____ are relations between word senses .

7. Both paraphrase and _____ are relations between sentence senses .

8. The relation between synonymy and paraphrase is parallel to the relation between _____ and _____ .

9. The relation between synonymy and hyponymy is parallel to the relation between _____ and _____ .

10. If A is a hyponym of B, B is a _____ of A .

11. Synonymy gives two _____ words .

12. Paraphrasing gives two _____ sentences .

13. Hyponymy is a relation between a _____ and a _____ .

CHAPTER 4

DISSIMILARITY OF SENSES

Words vary concerning the quality of their relations with one another . For example, *book* and *encyelopedia* are closely related; in fact, they belong to the same **semantic field** . In contrast, *book* and *fish* are not much related to each other : each belongs to a different semantic field .

In the previous chapter, Chapter 3, we have explained relations of **sense similarity** between words as shown in synonymy and hyponymy and sense similarity between sentences as shown in paraphrase and entailment . In this chapter, Chapter 4, we shall explain relations of **sense dissimilarity** between words and sense dissimilarity between sentences .

Antonymy

Look at these pairs of words :

1. alive, dead

2. sell, buy

3. hot, cold

4. north, east

5. north, south

6. cover, book

7. Saturday, Sunday

8. assistant professor, associate professor

9. cat, dog

If we examine the previous nine pairs, we find that each word in the pair excludes the other . If one is *alive,* he cannot be *dead* . The one who *sells* is not the one who *buys* . Something *hot* cannot be *cold* at the same time . Whatever is *north* cannot be *east* at the same time, and so on with the other pairs .

The sense relation between the two words of each previous pair is not that of synonymy or hyponymy . It is a **relation of antonymy,** i.e., oppositeness or at least dissimilarity . Antonymy, which is a sense relation between words, has nine different types, which we shall explain one by one in the following sections in this chapter .

Binary Antonymy

Look at these pairs :

1.male, female

2. alive, dead

3. bachelor, married

Each pair allows no third alternative . If one is a *male*, he is not a *female* . If one is *alive*, he cannot be *dead* . If one is *single*, he cannot be *married* at the same time .

Each word excludes and negates the other . *Alive* means *not dead*, *male* means *not female*, and *single* means *not married* . Such words are called **binary antonyms,** and the relation is called **binary antonymy** .

Some semanticists give this relation another name, i.e., **real antonymy,** because words here are extremely opposite to each other; it is the most antonymous antonymy . Some semanticists call this relation **complementary antonymy,** because the two words complete the circle : people are either *males* or *females, alive* or *dead, single* or *married* . Some linguists call this relation **extreme antonymy** for the same reason it has been called real antonymy .

Notice that such antonyms, i.e., binary antonymys, cannot be graded . They do not allow intensifiers or degree words such as *very, rather, fairly, somehow, somewhat* . We cannot say * *very married* or * *very dead*, for example . Such antonyms are ungradable . Therefore, this relation is also called **ungradable antonymy** .

To explain binary antonymy, we may put it this way : If A means – B, and B means – A, then A ↔ B, where – means *not*, and ↔ indicates antonymy . We may also put it this way :

$$A = _-B$$
$$B = _-A$$
$$\therefore A \leftrightarrow B$$

For example, if *male* means *not female,* and *female* means *not male, male* and *female* are antonyms .

In some cases, antonyms show quadrilateral relations . For example, humans are adult or non-adult, male or female . Let us see what comes out of such relations in Table 4 – 1 .

Table 4 – 1 : Quadrilateral Relations

	Male	**Female**
Adult	*man*	*woman*
Non-adult	*boy*	*girl*

This table allows some cases of antonymy, but it does not allow others . For instance, these are binary antonyms : *male / female, man / woman, boy / girl, adult / non-adult* . In contrast, *man / girl* and *woman / boy* are not binary antonyms . If you are asked about the opposite of *man,* you will say *woman,* not *girl* . Horizontal words in Table 4 – 1 are binary antonyms, but diagonal words are not .

Converse Antonymy

Look at these pairs :

1. sell, buy

2. teach, learn

65

3. father, son

4. give, receive

5. husband, wife

Such antonyms are called **converse antonyms,** and such relation is called **converse antonymy** or **converseness** . If *selling* occurs, *buying* occurs at the same time . If A *sells* B something, B *buys* it from A . If A *teaches* B, B *learns* from A . If A is the *father* of B, B is the *son* of A . If A *gives* to B, B *receives* from A . If A is the *husband* of B, B is the *wife* of A .

The two words of each pair are concomitant : no one can exist without the other . There is no *selling* without *buying*, no *father* without a *son*, and no *husband* without a *wife* .

Gradable Antonymy

Look at these pairs :

1. easy, difficult

2. cold, hot

3. near, far

4. clever, stupid

5. beautiful, ugly

Each previous pair can be represented by a scale of two extremes, allowing degrees in between . Notice that each word is gradable . For example, we can say *very easy, fairly easy, somehow easy, extremely easy* . The words of each pair are in gradable antonymy, and the words are **gradable antonyms** .

The difference between binary antonymy and gradable antonymy is that the first does not allow **gradability,** whereas the second does allow it . For example, we can grade *hot* and say *very hot, rather hot, fairly hot,* but we cannot say * *very married* or * *fairly married* .

Perpendicular Antonymy

Look at these pairs :

1. north, east

2. north, west

3. south, east

4. south, west

Such words refer to directions . Each word in each pair refers to a direction perpendicular to the other direction . For example, the *north* is perpendicular to the *east;* thus, *north* and *east* are in perpendicular antonymy, and the two words are **perpendicular antonyms** .

Extensional Antonymy

Look at these pairs :

1. north, south

2. east, west

3. right, left

4. up, down

The *north* is an extension of the *south* because both lie on the same extended line, unlike *north* and *west*, which are perpendicular to each other . Pairs (1 – 4) are in extensional anatomy, and the words of each pair are **extensional antonyms** or extensionally antonymous . Notice that both perpendicular antonymy and extensional antonymy are related to directions . Both of them can be called **directional antonymy .**

Partial Antonymy

Look at these pairs :

1. cover, book

2. brake, car

3. wall, room

4. finger, hand

5. pupil, eye

6. eardrum, ear

In every pair, we notice that the first word is a part of the second one, or, more accurately, the referent of the first word is part of the referent of the second word . for example, a *cover* is part of a *book*, a *brake* is a part of a *car*, and so on with the other pairs . Such a relation is called **partial antonymy,** and the two words of each pair are **partial antonyms** .

Notice that if A is a part of B, they are antonyms, because if a certain referent is A, it is not B, and if it is B, it is not A . For example, a *cover* is not a *book,* and a *book* is not a *cover* . They are related words, but each excludes the other .

In language expressions, such a relation can be structurally phrased in three ways . First, we can use the ***of*-structure,** e.g., *the finger of the hand, the pupil of the eye* . Notice that we cannot say * *the hand of the finger* .In the *of*-structures the part is the first word, and the whole is the second word . Second, we can use the **compound structure,** *e.g., book cover, room wall, car brake,* where the whole is the first word and the part is the second word . Notice that we cannot say * *cover book,* * *wall room,* or * *brake car* . Third, we can use the **genitive structure,** e.g., *the boy's hand,* where the whole is also the first word and the part is the second .

Cyclic Antonymy

Look at these groups :

1. *Saturday, Sunday, Monday, Tuesday, Wednesday, Thursday, Friday* .
2. *winter, spring, summer, autumn* .

Within each group, the sense relation is cyclic, not a linear relation . You can start anywhere and go in a circular or cyclic manner . If you start with *Saturday,* the week ends in *Friday* . If you start with *Monday,* the week ends in *Sunday* .

69

Each word in the group derives its sense from its position in the circle . For example, *spring* comes after *winter*, but before *summer* . *Thursday* comes after *Wednesday*, but before *Friday* .

Such words are in **cyclic antonymy,** and within each group the words are **cyclic antonyms** . Notice that *Saturday*, for example, is not necessarily the first day of the week; any day can be the first day . Similarly, any season can be chosen to be the first season in the year . The important thing is to keep the order within the cyclic group .

Rank Antonymy

Look at these groups :

1. assistant professor, associate professor, full professor .
2. freshman, sophomore, junior, senior .
3. Grade 1, Grade 2, Grade 3, . . . , Grade 12 .

The first group is the academic ranks of university professors, ending with the highest rank . The second group is university undergraduate years, beginning with the first year and ending with the fourth year . The third group is the school grades along the twelve years of study .

Each group consists of words or phrases with fixed order going from the lowest rank up to the highest rank . Such words within each group are in **rank antonymy,** and

70

they are **rank antonyms** . Such sense relation is also called **hierarchical antonymy** because words are statically ordered in a hierarchy .

Rank antonyms differ from cyclic antonyms in that rank antonyms are ordered linearly on a straight scale, which has the lowest beginning and the highest end, whereas cyclic antonyms are ordered in a circle, which has no specific beginning or end . Geometrically, the straight line has a beginning and an end, but the circle does not have either .

On the other hand, rank antonyms are similar to cyclic antonyms . The words of each group, whether of rank antonyms or cyclic antonyms, completely cover the related system . For example, the seven words *Saturday, Sunday, . . . , and Friday* cover the week system . The twelve words (or phrases) *Grade 1, Grade 2, . . ., Grade 12* cover the system of school years . Each group covers its related system, whether the group is in rank antonymy or cyclic antonymy .

Affinity Antonymy
Look at these groups :
1. apple, orange, banana
2. cow, sheep, horse
3. book, encyclopedia, magazine

In Group 1, the words are kinds of *fruit*, and, thus, each of them is a hyponym of *fruit* . In Group 2, each word is a hyponym of *domestic animals* . In Group 3, each word is a hyponym of *printed materials* .

Within each group, the words exclude one another . For example, if A is a *cow*, it cannot be a *sheep* or *horse* . Therefore, the words in each group are in **affinity antonymy,** and they are **affinity antonyms** . Such antonymy is called as such because the words of each group are related to one kind, and they are hyponyms of the same **superordinate** . For example, *cow, horse,* and *sheep* are all hyponyms of *domestic animals* .

Bilateral and Multiple Antonymy

If antonymy is a sense relation between two words only, it is called **bilateral antonymy** or **bi-antonymy** . Such antonymy applies to binary antonymy, gradable antonymy, converse antonymy, perpendicular antonymy, extensional antonymy, and partial antonymy . All these types of antonymy are relations between two words only .

In contrast, if antonymy is a sense relation between more than two words, it is called **multiple antonymy** . Such antonymy applies to rank antonymy, cyclic antonymy, and affinity antonymy . In some cases, antonymy may be between hundreds or thousands of words such as the different kinds of birds, animals, fishes, or plants . For the different types and classification of antonymy, see Figure 4 – 1 .

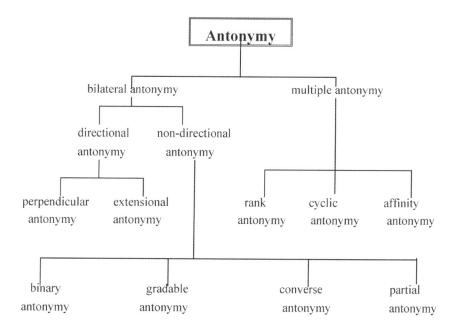

Figure 4 – 1 : Types of Antonymy

Contradictoriness

Look at these sentences :

1. Hani was born in 1975 .

2. Hani was born in 1985 .

These two sentences are **contradictories** of each other . The sense relation between them is called **contradictoriness** .

Two sentences (A and B) are in contradictoriness if they both cannot be true . The probabilities here concerning the truth and falsity of contradictories are these three :

1. A is true, and B is false .

2. A is false, and B is true .

3. A and B are false .

It cannot be that both contradictories, i.e., A and B, are true . Notice that contradictoriness is different from **contradiction,** which will be discussed in detail in Chapter 6 . The former is a sense relation between two S's, e.g., S's 1 and 2 . The latter is a sense property of one sentence having internal contradiction, e.g., *The cat is not an animal .*

Now we have six concepts, summarized in Table 4 – 2 .

Table 4 – 2 : Sense Relations

Relation Type	Relation between Words	Relation between Sentences	Sense Similarity	Sense Dissimilarity
1.Synonymy	+	—	+	—
2. Hyponymy	+	—	+	—
3. Antonymy	+	—	—	+
4. Paraphrase	—	+	+	—
5. Entailment	—	+	+	—
6. Contradictoriness	—	+	—	+

Antonymy-Contradictoriness Relationship

In Chapter 3, we discussed the relation between hyponymy and entailment . Is there a relation between antonymy and contradictoriness ? Let us see these sentences :

1. *This tree is an **apple** tree .*
2. *This tree is an **orange** tree .*
3. *Today is **Saturday** .*
4. *Today is **Sunday** .*
5. *This water is **hot** .*
6. *This water is **cold** .*

The words *apple* and *orange* in S's (1, 2) are affinity antonyms, and their antonymy makes S's (1, 2) in a contradictoriness relation, because the same tree cannot be an *apple* and *orange* tree at the same time . The words *Saturday* and *Sunday* in S's (3, 4) are cyclic antonyms, causing a contradictoriness relation between S's (3, 4) . Similarly, the words *hot* and *cold* in S's (5, 6) are gradable antonyms, leading to a contradictoriness relation between S's (5, 6) .

This shows that if two S's are identical in all words except two antonymous words in identical positions, the two S's will be contradictories of each other, provided that the referents are the same . In S's (1, 2), *this tree* in both S's must refer to the same tree; otherwise, the two S's will not be contradictories .

Look at these S's :

7. *The man bought a **goat**.*

8. *The man bought a **horse**.*

9. *Some people love to go to **France**.*

10. *Some people love to go to **Italy**.*

Although *goat* and *horse* in S's (7, 8) are affinity antonyms, the two S's are not contradictories, because both S's can be true : the man could buy a goat and a horse at the same time . In S's (9, 10), *France* and *Italy* are affinity antonyms as well, yet the two S's (9, 10) are not contradictories, because both sentences can be true at the same time .

We may conclude that antonymy does not always lead to contradictoriness . If two sentences are identical in all words except two antonyms in the same position and all referents in both S's are the same, the two S's may be contradictories . If R's are not the same, the two S's are not contradictories .

EXERCISES

Exercise 4 - 1

Is this antonymy binary (B) or gradable (G) ?

1. tall, short	_____	6. old, young	_____
2. wide, narrow	_____	7. true, false	_____

3. single, married _____   8. plus, minus   _____
4. winner, loser   _____   9. far, near   _____
5. man, woman   _____   10. come, go   _____

Exercise 4 - 2

Is this antonymy converse (C), gradable (G), or binary (B) ?

1. lend, borrow   _____   5. teacher, learner   _____
2.hard-working,lazy   _____   6. Paradise, Hell   _____
3. mother, son   _____   7. reward, punish   _____
4. husband, wife   _____   8. kind, cruel   _____

Exercise 4 - 3

Is this antonymy directional (D) or non-directional (ND) ?

1. right, left   _____   5. present, absent   _____
2. friend, enemy _____   6. south, east   _____
3. good, bad   _____   7. moral, immoral   _____
4. up, down   _____   8. objective, subjective _____

Exercise 4 - 4

Is this antonymy perpendicular (P) or extensional (E) ?

1. above, below   _____   5. northeast, southwest _____
2. over, under   _____   6. northwest, southwest _____
3. east, west   _____   7. north, south   _____
4. north, east   _____   8. south, east   _____

Exercise 4 - 5

Is this antonymy a rank (R), cyclic (C), or affinity (A) antonymy ?

1. July, August	_____	5. elementary school, intermediate school	_____
2. tiger, lion	_____	6. lily, tulip	_____
3. autumn, winter	_____	7. shark, dolphin	_____
4. Tuesday, Wednesday	_____	8. Grade 9, Grade 10	_____

Exercise 4 - 6

Is this antonymy bilateral (B) or multiple (M) ?

1. binary antonymy	_____	5. converse antonymy	_____
2. affinity antonymy	_____	6. gradable antonymy	_____
3. extensional antonymy	_____	7. cyclic antonymy	_____
4. rank antonymy	_____	8. perpendicular antonymy	_____

Exercise 4 - 7

What type of antonymy is shown by each pair ?

1. wide, narrow	_____	6. January, February	_____
2. north, south	_____	7. north, west	_____
3. sophomore, junior	_____	8. sheep, goat	_____
4. cardinal, ordinal	_____	9. sell, purchase	_____
5. seat, car	_____		

Exercise 4 - 8

Is each statement true (T) or false (F) ?

1. Antonymy includes contradictoriness .   _____

2. Binary antonymy is the opposite of gradable antonymy _____

3. *Southeast* and *southwest* are perpendicular antonyms . _____

4. *Northeast* and *southwest* are perpendicular antonyms . _____

5. If a group of words is in affinity antonymy, each word is a
   hyponym of a word labeling the group . _____

6. Converse antonymy is a non-directional antonymy . _____

7. Affinity antonymy is usually a bilateral antonymy . _____

8. Synonymy to paraphrase is like antonymy to
   contradictoriness . _____

9. Hyponymy to entailment is like contradictoriness to
   antonymy . _____

10. Contradictoriness is the same as contradiction . _____

Exercise 4 - 9

Give an antonym of each word .

1. right	_____	6. stop	_____
2. prevent	_____	7. lead	_____
3. five	_____	8. pleased	_____
4. truth	_____	9. forward	_____
5. trust	_____	10. moderation	_____

Exercise 4 - 10

**Fill in the blank with the missing word .
(A = Antonymy) .**

1. A can be bilateral or _____ .

2. A is a relation between _____ of words .

3. Contradictoriness is a sense relation between _____ .

4. A can be directional or _____ .

5. All types of A are ungradable except _____ A .

6. Directional A can be perpendicular or _____ .

7. The order of words is essential in _____ A .

8. Different animals are in affinity _____ .

CHAPTER 5

AMBIGUITY OF SENSES

A word or sentence is ambiguous if it has more than one sense . In this chapter, we shall explain the reasons and types of **ambiguity** of both words and sentences .

Look at these examples :

1. *fifteenth* : He is the fifteenth . Give me one fifteenth .

2. *fight* : to fight, a fight .

3. *file* : File it . Put it in a file .

4. *fill* : to fill a glass, fill a job, the fill of a hole .

5. *will* : He has enough will . He wrote his will .

6. *fire* : to set fire, to fire a gun, under fire, to fire questions at him, to fire an employee, to fire clay .

7. *firm* : strong, strict, company .

8. *pupil* : pupil at school, pupil of the eye .

9. *honeymoon* : to honeymoon, a honeymoon .

10. *side* : to side with, the two sides of the river .

11. *stage* : to stage a play, to stand on the stage, the stages of a process .

In the previous examples (1 – 11), each word has more than one sense, so they are **ambiguous words** . In fact, a large percentage of English words are ambiguous . If you open the dictionary and examine words and their senses, you will find that most words have more than one sense . *Webster's New Collegiate Dictionary,* for example, gives the word *pass* thirty-eight senses, *pound* ten senses, *swing* thirty senses, *sweep* seventeen senses, *sweat* twenty-three senses, and *type* eleven senses .

Homonymy

If a word has two senses or more with no relation between them, this would be a case of **homonymy** . In contrast, if the two senses are related, this would be a case of **polysemy** . Thus, word ambiguity is two types : homonymy and polysemy .

Let us see some examples of homonymy, where the senses of the same word are not related to each other :

1. *pen :* (a) *He wrote with a <u>pen</u> .*

  (b) *The sheep are in the <u>pen</u> .*

2. *file :* (a) *He kept the documents in the <u>file</u> .*

  (b) *He sharpened the knife with a <u>file</u> .*

3. *term :* (a) *The first school <u>term</u> was over .*

  (b) *What is the meaning of this <u>term</u> ?*

4. *steer :*   *(a) This <u>steer</u> was born one month ago .*

              (b) The captain is to <u>steer</u> the ship .

5. *moment :* *(a) This is a great <u>moment</u> in your life .*

              (b) The <u>moment</u> of force is a physics term .

6. *craft :*   *(a) He treated them with <u>craft</u> and deceit .*

              (b) This <u>craft</u> can carry ten passengers only .

7. *kind :*   *(a) He is a <u>kind</u> person .*

              (b) This is a new <u>kind</u> .

8. *type :*   *(a) She will <u>type</u> the letter .*

              (b) The suffix is one <u>type</u> of affixes .

If we examine the previous eight words, we notice that the two senses of each has no relation with each other . These are cases of homonymy . Of course, it is not always easy to decide whether the two senses are related or not . Sometimes the relation is there, but it may look so far or so weak that you hesitate to consider it a zero relation or to consider it a positive relation no matter how weak it is . For example, the word *wet* may mean *wet with rain* or *drunken* . Are the two senses related or not ? It is not always easy to decide .

Polysemy

Polysemy is a case of word which has two senses or more that are related to one another . In fact, in most cases, related senses are more frequent than unrelated senses . In other words, polysemy is probably more common than homonymy .

Let us see these examples of polysemy :

1. *chair :*   *(a) He sat on the <u>chair</u> .*

                 (b) He will <u>chair</u> the meeting .

2. *father :*   *(a) He is Ali's <u>father</u> .*

                 (b) He will <u>father</u> this child . (=adopt)

3. *fat :*   *(a) Avoid <u>fat</u> food .*

                 (b)He has a <u>fat</u> purse . (= full)

4. *civil :*   *(a) He studies <u>civil</u> engineering .*

                 (b) He spoke in a very <u>civil</u> way . (= polite)

5. *canary :*   *(a) The <u>canary</u> is a yellow bird .*

                 (b) She likes her <u>canary</u> dresses . (= yellow)

6. *blank :*   *(a) He signed a <u>blank</u> check .*

                 (b) Please, <u>blank</u> this line . (= erase)

7. *alloy :*   *(a) Brass is an <u>alloy</u> of copper and zinc .*

                 (b) Can you <u>alloy</u> these two metals ?

8. *depression :*   *(a) She is suffering <u>depression</u> .*

                 (b) The country was in a stage of economic <u>depression</u> .

9. *mend :*   *(a) The tailor <u>mended</u> the dress .*

                 (b) He <u>mended</u> the fire . (= give more coal)

10. *live :*   *(a) This wire is <u>live</u> .*

                 (b) This TV program is <u>live</u> .

Hundreds or thousands of such examples can be given to exemplify words with senses related to each other . Such words show cases of polysemy . If you examine the previous examples

(1 – 10), you can easily see how the two senses of each word are closely related .

Homonymy and Synonymy

Hononymy is a case of sense ambiguity caused by a word having two senses or more . In contrast, synonymy is a case where two different words have the same sense, e.g., *deep, profound* .

Homonymy involves one word, but synonymy involves two words . In homonymy one word has two senses, but in synonymy two words have the same sense .

Is it possible to define homonymy using synonymy ? Yes, it is . Homonymy is a case of a word having two synonyms none of which is a synonym of the other . In other words, homonymy is a case of a word that has two non-synonymous synonyms or senses .

As for polysemy, a similar definition can be given . The only difference between homonymy and polysemy is that the senses of homonymy are not related, whereas the senses in the case of polysemy are closely related . Notice that the senses involved in both homonymy and polysemy can be not only two senses, but sometimes more than two .

This table, Table 5 – 1, shows the relations between homonymy, polysemy, and synonymy . This table is a good summary of related information about these three concepts .

Table 5 – 1 : Homonymy, Polysemy, and Synonymy

Aspect	Homonymy	Polysemy	Synonymy
1. one word involved	+	+	—
2. two words involved	—	—	+
3. sense similarity	—	—	+
4. sense ambiguity	+	+	—
5. two related senses	—	+	—
6. two unrelated senses	+	—	—
7. one word with two senses	+	+	—
8. two words with one sense	—	—	+

Accounting for Polysemy and Homonymy

Why do words have more than one sense ? Basically, a word should have one sense only so that ambiguity may have no place . How can polysemy and homonomy be explained or accounted for ? One may present different explanations for this phenomenon :

1. **Economy** . It is obvious that senses are more in number than words in all languages . English has about one million words now . If each word had had one sense, English would have had about five million words . Thus, polysemy becomes an economic way of using language; one word is made to convey more than sense . It is a means to increase word efficiency and minimize the number of words in a language .

2. **Coincidence** . If a word has two unrelated senses, the only possible explanation here is mere coincidence . How else can one explain homonymy in a word like *file* ? Homonymy is obviously an accidental phenomenon .

3. **Noun-Verb function** . Many English nouns are also used as verbs without any affixation; the same word is used as a noun and as a verb with two clearly related senses . Examples are *export, import, man, ship, cushion, carpet, cut, fancy, fan, mud, school, insult, respect, water, rest, shape,* and *face* .

4. **Transitive-Intransitive function** . The same verb form may function transitively or intransitively, resulting in two related senses for the same word, which makes a case of polysemy . Examples are *move, melt, increase, decrease, shape,* and *walk* .

Sentence Ambiguity

As said before, a word is ambiguous if it has two senses or more that are not synonymous with one another . Similarly, a sentence is ambiguous if it has two senses or more that are not paraphrases of one another .

Look at these sentences :
1. *Please, give me the file .*
2. *The pupil needs some care .*
3. *Visiting relatives can be boring .*
4. *He ate five oranges and apples .*

Each sentence (1 – 4) is ambiguous because it has two senses . The ambiguity of S_1 is caused by the ambiguity of *file*, and the ambiguity of S_2 is caused also by the ambiguity of *pupil* (*of the eye or of the school*) . Here, in S's (1 – 2), sentence ambiguity is caused by word ambiguity . Such sentence ambiguity is called **lexical ambiguity** .

In contrast, S's (3 – 4) are ambiguous not because of word ambiguity, but because of **grammatical ambiguity** . S_3 either indicates *to visit relatives* or *relatives who visit* . S_4 is ambiguous because *five* has two relations with the nouns after : Is *five* the number of oranges and apples together or the number of oranges only ? Grammatical ambiguity is also called **structural ambiguity** or *syntactic ambiguity* .

Word Ambiguity and Sentence Ambiguity

What is the relation between word ambiguity (WA) and sentence ambiguity (SA) ? To answer this question, let us examine these sentences :

1. *Put these documents in the **file** .*

2. *Where is the **file** ?*

3. *The chicken is ready to eat .*

Although S_1 has an ambiguous word, i. e., *file*, the S is not ambiguous . As for S_2, it is ambiguous because it has an ambiguous word, which is *file* . Concerning S_3, it is ambiguous although it has no ambiguous words .

Therefore, to explain the relation between WA and SA, we have these different cases :

1. WA may sometimes cause SA, e.g., S_2 .

2. WA may not cause SA, e.g., S_1 .

3. SA may exist without WA, e.g., S_3 .

4. Ambiguous words do not always make ambiguous S's, e.g., S_1.

Grammatical Ambiguity

Grammatical ambiguity (GA), sometimes called structural or **syntactic ambiguity**, implies that a sentence has two senses neither of which is a paraphrase of the other, i.e., two different senses, provided that such ambiguity is caused by the grammatical structure of the sentence, not by an ambiguous word in that sentence .

Grammatical ambiguity (GA) may have different causes such as :

1. The ***and* structure** may cause GA, e.g., *He saw three boys and girls* . It may be *three (boys and girls)* or *(three boys) and girls* .

2. The **prepositional-phrase structure** may cause GA if it may modify or be related to more than one word in the sentence, e.g., *He saw the man with the telescope* . This S may mean either that *he used the telescope to see the man* or *that he saw the man who was carrying a telescope* .

3. The **verb voice** may cause GA, e.g., *The bird is ready to eat* . The verb *to eat* may be active, which gives one sense, or passive, i.e., *to be eaten,* which gives another sense .

4. The *–ing* **form** may cause GA, e.g., *Flying planes can be dangerous* .The *–ing* form can be a present participle functioning as a premodifier or a gerund functioning as a noun .

5. The **possessive form** may cause GA, e.g., *John's paintings* . It could be that *John is the owner of the paintings* or *he is the painter himself* .

6. The *or* **structure** may cause GA, e.g., *This can be A or B* . The grammatical word *or* could be understood to be an option between A and B, which are two words for the same sense . The other probable sense is that it can be either A or B, which are two different words not indicating the same sense .

7. The **premodification structure** may cause GA if there are many premodifiers before a noun, e.g., *the acquired language output,* where *acquired* may premodify *language* or *output* .

Sentence Ambiguity and Paraphrase

Can we define sentence ambiguity (SA) in terms of paraphrase ? Yes, we can . SA is a case of a sentence having two paraphrases neither of which is a paraphrase of the other .

If a sentence has two different paraphrases or two different senses, each of which is not a paraphrase of the other paraphrase, this sentence is ambiguous, whether lexically or grammatically . Symbolically, it may be expressed this way :

$A \equiv B$

$A \equiv C$

$B \not\equiv C$

$\therefore$ A is an ambiguous sentence .

If sentence A is a paraphrase of sentence B, sentence A is a paraphrase of sentence C, and B is not a paraphrase of C, then A is an ambiguous sentence .

EXERCISES

Exercise 5 - 1

Are these words ambiguous (A) or unambiguous (U) ? Refer to the dictionary if necessary .

1. dish	_____	7. feature	_____
2. fate	_____	8. feast	_____
3. fast	_____	9. back	_____
4. feel	_____	10. jump	_____
5. smell	_____	11. hydrogen	_____
6. morpheme	_____	12. zinc	_____

Exercise 5 - 2

Give two senses of each word . You may refer to the dictionary .

1. well _____ _____

2. tick _____ _____

3. ruler   _____   _____

4. standard   _____   _____

5. stand   _____   _____

6.earth   _____   _____

7. pay   _____   _____

8. miss   _____   _____

9. element   _____   _____

10. share   _____   _____

Exercise 5 - 3

Is the relation between the word senses a case of homonymy (H) or polysemy (P) ?

1. *fast :*   *(a) He will **fast** this week .*

               *(b) He went **fast** .*   _____

2. *ring :*   *(a) **Ring** him now .*

               *(b) **Ring** the bell .*   _____

3. *remember :* *(a) He was to **remember** everything .*

               *(b) You have to **remember** the waiter .*   _____

4. *shape :*   *(a) You are in good **shape** now .*

               *(b) You can **shape** it as you wish .*   _____

5. *mature :*   *(a) He is a **mature** person .*

               *(b) It is a **mature** apple .*   _____

6. *plane :*   *(a) The **plane** will leave soon .*

               *(b) The table has a **plane** surface .*   _____

7. *list :*   *(a) He read the **list** .*

               *(b) He corrected the **list** of the ship .*   ———

8. pen :   (a) He wrote with a **pen** .

(b) The goats are in the **pen** .   _____

9. phrase :   (a) This **phrase** must be modified .

(b) You have to **phrase** it differently .   _____

10. sage :   (a) He is a **sage** man .

(b) This **sage** may be useful to you .   _____

Exercise 5 - 4

Is each sentence ambiguous (A) or not (N) . If it is ambiguous, what kind of ambiguity is it : lexical ambiguity (LA) or grammatical ambiguity (GA) ?

1. He couldn't swallow it .   _____ _____

2. Where is the tip ?   _____ _____

3. Write your name here .   _____ _____

4. It has a large trunk .   _____ _____

5. Have you seen his drawings ?   _____ _____

6. He ate three apples and oranges .   _____ _____

7. It may cause X or Y .   _____ _____

8. Have you seen the mug ?   _____ _____

9. She drove the car very fast .   _____ _____

10. I saw him in the garden .   _____ _____

Exercise 5 - 5

These sentences are grammatically ambiguous . What are the two senses of each ?

1. Parents' help is very necessary .

     a. —————————————————————

     b.—————————————————————

2. They produce dry fruit and vegetables .

     a. —————————————————————

     b. —————————————————————

3. He bought modern books and novels .

     a.—————————————————————

     b.—————————————————————

4. Visiting patients may cause problems .

     a.—————————————————————

     b. —————————————————————

5. He hit the thief with the stick .

     a.—————————————————————

     b.—————————————————————

Exercise 5 - 6

Examine the S's of Exercise 5 – 5, and decide on the type of grammatical structure that has caused the ambiguity .

1. _____

2. _____

3. _____

4. _____

5. _____

CHAPTER 6

THE TYPES OF MEANING

Meaning is the essence of communication . This communication requires that people agree among themselves on the meanings of words . If such agreement does not exist, communication becomes almost impossible . Suppose that you said, " Man needs water and food ." If the hearer asks you about the meaning of *man, need, water,* and *food,* you will find it very difficult or in fact impossible to continue your conversation with him . If, in explaining *water,* you tell him that *water* is a liquid whose molecule consists of hydrogen and oxygen, and he begins to ask about the meaning of each word you say (what do you mean by liquid, molecule, oxygen, etc.), you will certainly come to the conclusion that such a conversation with that hearer will be utterly useless and communication is obviously impossible .

Analytical Meaning and Synthetic Meaning

Look at these sentences :

1. *The elephant is an animal .*
2. *Lettuce is a kind of vegetables .*

3. The bachelor is an unmarried man .

4. The widow is a woman whose husband is dead .

5. The woman is a female .

6. A door is an entrance place .

7. John is forty years old .

8. The distance between the earth and the sun is 93 million miles.

9. The world has more than 3000 languages .

10. His father is a lawyer .

11. Salim's cumulative average is 79 .

If we examine S's (1 – 6), we find that each S is true by itself, internally true, true by the nature of relations of words inside the S . The elephant (S₁), for example, is an animal by definition; there is no elephant which is not an animal . We do not need external investigation to verify the truth of these S's . Such S's are called **analytical sentences** and their meaning is an **analytical meaning** .

In contrast, S's (7-11) cannot be judged for truth or falsity depending on the internal language (L) of the S . For example, we cannot decide the truth of S7 just by reading this S; we have to investigate its truth outside the S itself . There is nothing in the S itself that proves it is false or true . Such S's are called **synthetic sentences** . They can be true if they match reality or false if they do not .

The analytical S is always true, whereas the synthetic S can be true or false .

Contradiction

Look at these sentences (S's) :

1. The elephant is not an animal .

2. Lettuce is not a vegetable .

3. The bachelor is not an unmarried man .

4. The widow is not a woman whose husband is dead .

5. The woman is not a female .

6. A door is not an entrance place .

These S's (1-6) are a negation of the first six S's (1-6) under the previous sub-heading, which are analytical S's . If you negate an analytical S, the result is a **contradiction** . Since the analytical S is always true, its negation is always false . This implies that the contradiction is always false .

If we examine S's (1-6), we find out that they are all necessarily false . Their falsity can be easily verified, not through checking the external world, but through the internal relations of the words inside the S itself . For example, in S_5, a woman by definition is a female : femininity is an essestial feature of *woman* . Since the analytical S is always true, and since the contradiction is a negation of the analytical S, the contradition, as a result, is always false .

As we can change an analytical S into a contradiction through negation, similarly we can change a contradiction to an analytical S .

7. *The cat is not an animal*
    ⇒ *The cat is an animal*
8. *The cat is a plant .*
    ⇒ *The cat is not a plant .*

Changing a contradiction into an analytical S can be done in two ways . First, if the contradiction is negative, omit the negator, and the result will be an analytical S, as in S_7 . Second, if the contradiction is affirmative, add a negator, and the result will be an analytical S, as in S_8 .

Finally, as far as information is concerned, we notice that both the analytical S and the contradiction S are not informative S's because neither gives the hearer any additional information about the world . The only S that can inform is the synthetic S if it is a true one . In addition, the features of **analyticity,** syntheticity, and contradiction are features of S's, not words .

Lexical and Grammatical Meanings

On the sentence level, the meaning (M) of the sentence consists of words and grammar . Words give the **lexical meaning** and grammar gives the grammatical meaning, which consists of the morphological M and the syntactic M, e.g., *The man killed the lion.*

Let us discuss the three types of meaning :

1. **Lexical meaning** . It is that part of sentence meaning (SM) provided by its words or **lexemes** . If a word in a S is replaced by another non-synonymous word, the SM will change . The more words are replaced in the S, the larger the change in SM will be . This proves the significance of words in SM .

2. **Morphological meaning** . It is part of the grammatical M, and it is mainly influenced by prefixes, infixes, derivational suffixes, and inflectional suffixes taken by the word . A famous example like *The vapy coops dasaked the citars molently* can prove the point . Although this S does not have real English words, and, thus, it has no lexical M, the suffixes make this S have some kind of M; we can understand something from this non-understandable S : *The citars were dasaked by the vapy coops in a molent way* . Upon hearing this S, one feels that *someone did something to someone in a certain way* .

3. **Syntactic meaning** . It is part of the grammatical M, and it is mainly determined by word order inside the S . The S *The lion killed the man* has the same words as the S *The man killed the lion,* yet the two S's have different M's, a difference caused by syntax, i.e., word order .

Meaning and Context

The word influences the meaning of the S, and the S influences the meaning of the word . In other words, the word meaning is sometimes or often determined by context . Such a word meaning is called the **contextual meaning .** While reading, we often understand a certain word to have a certain M; then as we go on reading, we find that that word has another M different from the meaning we have understood first .

In fact, most words have more than one meaning, a fact that can be easily verified if you open the dictionary and have a look at its entries . You rarely find a word with one meaning only . Which meaning is meant is usually determined by the context of the S or the situation of the U .

Look at the different meanings of *see* in these S's :
1. *The doctor **sees** him every week .*
2. *Do you **see** the tree there ?*
3. ***See** him to his home .*
4. *Do you **see** what I mean ?*
5. *He will **see** you tomorrow .*

The verb *see* has a different M in each S : *examine, perceive with the eye, accompany, understand,* and *visit,* respectively . These examples prove the point of contextual meanings .

Meaning and External Factors

The meaning (M) of a sentence (S) is not only determined by its words and its grammar, but by external factors as well . The same S can mean different things in different situations or on different occasions . Here are some of these **external factors,** which may be also called **situational factors** :

1. **Body movements .** When a person speaks, he may move his hand(s), head, fingers, eyes, shoulders, neck, and body . Such movements may emphasize the speech message, but they may sometimes contradict it . The S says something, but body movements may say something else .

2. **Facial feelings .** The face of the speaker usually shows a lot of feelings accompanying speech, such as sorrow, regret, eagerness, blame, threat, anger, weakness, pity, sympathy, and reproach . Such feelings and emotions show themselves easily on the face and especially in the eyes, the mirror of the psyche, as they are often described . These facial feelings may reinforce what the sentence says or may contradict it and thus affect the sentence meaning (SM) .

3. **Tone .** The speaker's tone may reveal his actual feelings, and, consequently, plays a role in the SM .

4. **Conversers' roles .** Any conversation requires at least two conversers : a speaker and a hearer, who normally exchange

101

the acts of speaking and hearing . The SM is strongly affected by the conversers' roles : who is speaking to whom . Such roles could be teacher / student, husband / wife, father / son, mother / daughter, friend / friend, employer / employee, or vice versa . The same S may have different meanings (M's), depending on who said what to whom . A question like " *Why are you late ?* " said by a friend to a friend may not require an answer, but the same question said by the teacher to his student does require an answer .

5. **Previous relations** . Another external factor that affects the SM is the previous relations between the conversers : Is it a friendly relation or an antagonistic relation ? The same S can trigger different responses, depending on the ex-relations between the two conversers .

6. **Physical environment** . The conversers need not mention everything explicitly in their conversation . The physical environment itself can facilitate their communication, and many deictic words can be used such as *here, there, this, that, these, those, now* .

Relative Meaning

All languages have relative words with relative meanings, e.g., *near, far, small, large, heavy, light, easy, difficult, tall, and short* . This relativity appears in several ways :

1. The judgment about such words differs from one individual to another . What is *near* in your opinion may be *far* in another person's opinion, for example .

2. The meaning of such words differs from time to time . What you judge as *heavy* now may be judged as *light* by you yourself later . Your judgment partly depends on your psychological mood and on the situation in general .

3. The meaning of such words is partly dependent on what is being modified . For example, a *small* elephant is very much larger than a *large* mouse .

It may be noticed that such words are not only adjectives . They can be nouns as well, e.g., *nearness, farness, smallness, largeness, easiness, difficulty, tallness, and shortness* . Most relative words indicate distance, length, weight, number, or size, all of which are some kinds of measurement .

Psychological Meaning

A word usually has a *basic meaning*, i.e., the dictionary meaning . It is an objective common M shared by all native speakers of a certain L .

However, some words have an additional psychological meaning or **emotional meaning** e.g., *home, father, mother, friendship, son,* and *brother* . Objectively, the *father* is the male parent, but psychologically, *father* is, of course, much more than a male parent, for instance .

The psychological meaning of a word may be general, i.e., common to all native speakers of a certain L, e.g., the meaning of words such as *father, brother* . It may be special as well, i.e., dependent on a certain person's experience . For example, a *dog* will be a horrible symbol to a child once bitten by a dog .

Psychological meanings may be positive if they are attached to emotions like loyalty, tenderness, friendship, brotherhood, happiness, satisfaction, and pleasure . They may also be negative if they are attached to emotions like disloyalty, deceit, fear anger, distress, and sadness .

Literal Meaning and Figurative Meaning

Look at these two S's :

1. They cornered him, and he couldn't run away .

2. They cornered him, and he couldn't deny .

The same sentence may have two meanings : one is literal, and the other is figurative . For example, in the first sentence (S_1), the cornering is literal : they chased him, and finally he was in the corner unable to run away . In S_2, there is no chasing, nor is there a real corner . S_1 has a literal meaning, whereas S_2 has a figurative one .

The **figurative meaning** applies to most, if not all, proverbs used in all languages . Here are some examples :

3. All roads lead to Rome .

4. A stich in time saves nine .

5. As you sow, so shall you reap .

6. The empty barrel makes a lot of noise .

When any of these proverbs is used, it is used figuratively . S_3 is used when there are no roads and no Rome; S_4, no stiches; S_5, no sowing or reaping; S_6, no barrels, neither solid nor empty . All these proverbs have figurative meanings and have lost their original literal meanings .

Meaning and Definition

How can we define a word meaning ? There are several ways to do that :

1. **Descriptive definition** . We can define by describing what is to be defined . For example, *a whale is the largest sea animal whose length may reach thirty meters and whose width may reach six meters* .

2. **Functional definition.** Here we define by explaining the function . For example, *a preposition is a word that precedes the noun and puts it in the accusative case* .

3. **Demonstrative definition** . Here we define by demonstration, i.e., pointing to the referent .

4. **Ordinal definition** . Here we define by showing the position or rank . For example, *Saturday comes after Friday and before Sunday* .

5. **Synonymous definition** . Here we define by giving the synonym, e.g., *wealthy* as the synonym of *rich* .

6. **Antonymous definition** . Here we define by giving the antonym, e.g., *wealthy* as the opposite of *poor* .

7. **Hyponymous definition** . Here we define by showing the hyponymous relationship between two words, e.g., *apple* as a kind of *fruit* .

Meaning and Stereotype

For the descriptive definition to be adequate, it must be so comprehensive that it includes all necessary qualities and so restrictive that it excludes other R's . For example, if we define a *square* as a figure of four sides, this definition will not be adequate because it consists of two qualities only, i,e., figure and four sides, which are not enough to distinguish a *square* from other four-side figures such as the *rectangle* and the *parallelogram* .

Thus, an adequate **descriptive definition** must be an exclusive one . Back to the example of the *square*, its definition should be this : *it is a plane figure, with four equal sides, four* *right angles, and two equal perpendicular diagonals* . Such a definition applies to squares only and excludes any figures that are not squares .

A descriptive definition must include all **necessary qualities** . It is a complete list of all typical qualities of the referent (R) . Such a list can be called a **stereotype** .

For a review, let us see the differences between these four terms, i.e., extension, prototype, sense, and stereotype :

1. The extension is a group of all potential R's, but the prototype is an actual one of them .

2. The extension is concrete, but sense is an abstract relationship between expressions in the same L .

3. The prototype is concrete, but the stereotype is abstract .

4. The stereotype and sense are abstract, but the extension and prototype are concrete .

5. The extension and sense cover all related cases, but the prototype and stereotype cover typical cases only .

Basic and Secondary Meanings

Every word has a dictionary meaning agreed on by all native speakers of a certain L . Such a meaning may be also called the **conceptual meaning** . However, many words have another meaning added to the basic meaning, which may be called the **secondary meaning** or the additional meaning, which comes to our attention from time to time especially when we make a simile .

Look at these sentences :
1. *They behaved like <u>sheep</u> . (submissive)*
2. *He was like a <u>rabbit</u> . (coward)*
3. *They fought like <u>lions</u> . (courageous)*
4. *She was like a <u>bee</u> . (active)*
5. *He was a <u>butcher</u> . (very cruel)*
6. *This shop is like a <u>pharmacy</u> . (expensive)*
7. *She is like a <u>rose</u> . (beautiful)*
8. *He is like <u>Einstein</u> . (genius)*

The basic meaning of *sheep* does not include *submissive,* which is a secondary meaning of the word . So is the case with the other seven underlined words, each of which conveys an **additional meaning** not already exsistent in its basic meaning .

Stylistic Meaning

Many words convey a meaning that indicates the stylistic level of the word . Such meaning is called the stylistic meaning, which shows whether the word is formal, standard, colloquial, slang, poetic, or terminological .

For example, *aunt* is more formal than *auntie* .
Look at these pairs of words : *center / nucleus, side / margin,*
show / indicate, explain / illustrate, dad / father, important /
significant, chat / conversation, word / lexeme, sound / phone . If
we examine each pair, we can easily find that the first word is
less formal than the second . This **formality level** of the word is
carried by its **stylistic meaning** .

Echoich Meaning

Some words show a part of their meaning in their phonetic
form . Such words are usually called **onomatopoeic words,**
e.g., *buzz, splash, murmur, whisper, whiz, mew, roar,* and such
a meaning is called the **echoic meaning** or the **phonetic**
meaning .

Such words exist in all L's although they are few in
number . The general rule is that most words do not show a
justifiable relation between their phonetic forms and their
meanings; such relation is usually an arbitrary one . Why is a
book called a *book,* a door a *door,* or a chair a *chair* ? There is
no obvious reason at all .

Semantic Units

Which language units have meaning, and which ones do
not ? Language units, graded from the lowest to the highest, are
the phoneme, syllable, morpheme, word, phrase, clause, and

finally the sentence . The phoneme lies at the bottom of the hierarchy, and the sentence lies at the top .

As for meaning, the phoneme and syllable are meaningless units, whereas the others are meaningful . The smallest meaningful unit is the **morpheme,** which may be bound or free and which may be a **base** or an **affix** . The affix may be a prefix, infix, or suffix . Morphemes combine together to make a word, e.g., *visualization* (visu + al + ize + tion) . Words combine to make a phrase, e.g., *the + large + book* . Phrases combine to make a clause or a sentence, e.g., *He + read + all the large book* .

Meaning and Parts of Speech

Is there a relationship between meaning and parts of speech ? In traditional grammar, parts of speech, or at least some of them, have been defined mainly according to meaning . For example, a noun has been defined as a word referring to a person, animal, thing, place, time, or event . The verb has been defined as a word referring to an action in the past, present, or future .

Such definitions are semantically oriented; we can label them as **semantic definitions** . That is why modern grammarians have objected to these definitions . They argue that, in grammar, parts of speech should have either morphological definitions or syntactic definitions . **Morphological definitions** depend on inflectional and derivational suffixes taken by the word, and **syntactic definitions** depend on the positional function of the word as used in a certain sentence .

The neo-grammarians' view is justifiable and defendable . In semantics, terms should be defined semantically, not syntactically . In morphology, terms should be defined morphologically . In syntax, terms should be defined syntactically, not semantically .

Meaning and Roles

Look at these sentences :
1. *The <u>boy</u> opened the door with the key .*
2. *The <u>door</u> was opened with the key by the <u>boy</u> .*
3. *The <u>key</u> opened the door .*
4. *The boy wrote a <u>letter</u> .*
5. *The <u>day</u> of graduation has come .*
6. *This is the <u>site</u> of the battle .*
7. *He went to <u>school</u> .*

Examining the previous S's, we notice that *boy* in S₁ is a subject according to syntax, but an *agent* of the action according to semantics . In S₂, *door* is a subject (in syntax), but a *recipient* (in semantics) . In S₃, *key* is also a subject (in syntax), but an *instrument* of the action (in semantics) .

In addition, *letter* in S$_4$ is a direct object (in syntax), but a *result* of the action (in semantics) . In S$_5$, *day* is a subject (in syntax), but a *time* (in semantics) . In S$_6$, *site* is a subject attribute or subject complement (in syntax), but a *location* (in semantics) . In S$_7$, *school* is a prepositional complement (in syntax), but a *goal* (in semantics) .

Thus, terms such as subject, object, subject complement, and prepositional complement are grammatical or syntactic terms that depend on the word position or function in the sentence . Such terms are of little or no use in semantics, which requires the usage of its own terms, which depend on meaning and not on position or syntactic function .

Semantics, which is the study of meaning, has these terms which are completely dependent on meaning :

1. **Agent** . It is the doer of the action, regardless of its position in the S, e.g., *boy* in S$_2$.

2. **Recipient** . It is the receiver of the action, regardless of its position in the S, e.g., *door* in S$_2$.

3. **Result** . It is the result of the action, e.g., *letter* in S$_4$.

4. **Time** . It is what indicates the time of the action, regardless of position, e.g., *day* in S$_5$.

5. **Location** . It is what indicates the place of the action, regardless of position, e.g., *site* in S$_6$.

6. **Instrument** . It is what indicates the instrument of the action, regardless of position, e.g., *key* in S's 1 – 3 .

7. **Goal** . It is what the agent aims at, e.g., *school* in S$_7$.

The seven previous roles are merely semantic roles because they completely depend on meaning with disregard to positions in the sentence . These **semantic roles** are obviously different from **syntactic terms** . The *subject* is not the *agent;* the *object* is not the *recipient;* the *adverb of time* is not the *time;* the *adverb of place* is not the *location* .

EXERCISES

Exercise 6 - 1

Are these sentences analytical S's (A), synthetic S's (S), or contradictions (C) ?

1. The Pacific Ocean is the largest ocean .

2. The widow is a woman whose husband is dead .

3. His father is his male parent.

4. Fishes live in water .

5. His mother is fifty years old .

6. His mother is not his female parent .

Exercise 6 -2

Are these statements true (T) or false (F) ?

1. The analytical S is always true .

2. The synthetic S is not true .

3. The analytical S is internally true .

4. If the synthetic S is true, it is externally so .

5. If the analytical S is negated, it becomes a contradiction .

6. A contradiction is sometimes true .

7. If we omit the negator of a contradiction, it becomes a synthetic S .

8. The synthetic S is informative, but the analytical S is not .

9. If a contradiction is affirmative, adding a negator to it makes it a synthetic S .

10. The sentence meaning (SM) is determined by its words only .

11. The S has three meanings combined together : lexical M, morphological M, and syntactic M .

Exercise 6 - 3

What is the contextual meaning of the underlined word ? Give another possible meaning outside the context .

1. He will come after this _fall_ .

2. He knows three _tongues_ .

3. This sentence has _sense_ .

4. A lot of water comes from this _spring_ .

Exercise 6 - 4

What external factors affect the sentence meaning (SM) ?

1. _____   4. _____

2. _____   5. _____

3. _____   6. _____

Exercise 6 - 5

Which word or words in each group have a relative meaning ?

1. large , small, child, student   _____

2. engineer, doctor, tall, car   _____

3. city, few, glass, school   _____

4. warm, driver, table, flower   _____

Exercise 6 - 6

Define each as required between brackets .

1. ship (descriptively) :   _____

2. conjunction (functionally) :   _____

3. window (demonstratively) :   _____

4. Tuesday (ordinally) :   _____

5. courageous (synonym) :   _____

6. rich (antonym) :   _____

7. apple (hyponym) :   _____

Exercise 6 - 7

Are these statements true (T) or false (F) ?

1. The stereotype is the prototype . _____

2. Both the stereotype and sense are abstract . _____

3. Both the stereotype and extension are abstract . _____

4. The stereotype is the same as sense . _____

Exercise 6 - 8

What is the secondary meaning that may be conveyed by each word (in addition to its basic meaning) ?

1. mother _____

2. father _____

3. brother _____

4. soldier _____

Exercise 6 - 9

Which word in each group has an echoic meaning ?

1. road, murmur, street, building _____

2. puff, river, wave, sea _____

3. smile, head, heart, crush _____

4. surface, moon, squeak, horizon _____

Exercise 6 - 10

Which type is the bold-type unit : morpheme, word, phrase, or sentence ?

1. He is ready . _____

116

2. They are **honest** people .   _____

3. He is **at the meeting** .   _____

4. She learns quickly .   _____

Exercise 6 - 11

What is the semantic role of the bold-type word ?

1. He cut the **rope** with a knife .   _____

2. The **knife** cut the rope .   _____

3. **Hani** cut the rope .   _____

4. The carpenter made a **table** .   _____

5. This is the **year** of victory .   _____

6. He flew to **Paris** .   _____

CHAPTER 7

THE ANALYSIS OF MEANING

Every word has a sense . The **sense** of a word is the relations of the word with other words in the same language . Such relations are synonymy, hyponymy, and antonymy . Each sentence has a sense, which consists of the sentence relations with other sentences in the same language . Such relations are paraphrase, entailment, and contradictoriness, as was explained in the previous chapters .

In addition, each word has a meaning . What is meaning ? The meaning of a word is the total of the **semantic features** of that word .

Word From

A word has a form, a distribution, and a meaning . The word form is two types : a spoken form and a written form . The **spoken form** consists of phones horizontally concatenated . This form is also called the *phonetic form*, the *oral form*, or the *audible form;* it is what we say and hear . The **written form** consists of horizontally strung graphemes . It is also called the *graphic form* or the **readable form;** it is what we write and read .

Word Distribution

Every word has a distribution, which determines how to use the word . This distribution is two kinds : grammatical and stylistic . The **grammatical distribution** of the word determines the class or category of the word : a noun, pronoun, adjective, verb, adverb, preposition, article, cardinal, ordinal, determiner, conjunction, or interjection . These word classes determine how the word can be used functionally in larger units such as phrases, clauses, and sentences .

Each word, in addition, has a **stylistic distribution** . This distribution determines when and where to use the word : in prose or poetry, in speech or writing, in formal or informal usage, in the standard dialect or a colloquial dialect .

As said before, each word has a meaning, which is the most delicate component of the word . People usually do not disagree on the word form (pronunciation or spelling); nor do they disagree on its distribution . The delicate component of the word is not the form or distribution; it is meaning . What is more delicate than meaning is the meaning of meaning . This issue is one of the main issues studied by semantics : what is meaning and what is the meaning of meaning ?

Meaning of Meaning

What is meaning ? What is the meaning of meaning ? What are the elements or components of meaning ? For example, what makes a tree a tree ? What makes an apple an apple ? What distinguishes an apple from an orange ? What are the semantic features of a word ? These features combine together to make a word with a specific meaning differing from other words .

Semantic Features

Semantic features can be also called **semantic components,** semantic elements, or semantic determiners . If we want to analyze a word meaning, we have to analyze it into its semantic features . For example, what are the semantic features of *boy* ? The word *boy* is + living, + male, + young, + human . Notice that we use only those features that can be **distinctive features** . When we analyze *boy*, we exclude features like + solid, + weight, + size . For every word, we choose only those related, distinctive, and significant features .

Notice that semantic features entail one another . For example, *boy* is + noun . Since nouns can be + living (like *man, girl, child*) or – living (like *table, door, chair*), we have to describe *boy* as + living . Since living beings can be + human or – human, *boy* is to be described as + human . Since humans can be males or females, *boy* has to be described as + male . Since males are either young or not, *boy* has to be described as + young .

We can think of dozens of distinctive semantic features . Examples are ∓ living, ∓ male, ∓ human, ∓ masculine, ∓ young, ∓ edible, ∓ drinkable, ∓ sweet, ∓ concrete, ∓ visible, ∓ printed, ∓ countable, ∓ proper, ∓ static, and ∓ neutral . The word *book*, for example, is – living, Ø male, – human, Ø masculine, Ø young, – edible, – drinkable, Ø sweet, + concrete, + visible, + printed, + countable, – proper, Ø static, + neutral . We use + for *positive*, – for *not*, and Ø for *not applicable* . For symbols, see Appendix I at the end of this book .

Types of Semantic Features

There are four types of semantic features :

1. **Positive feature** or plus feature . It is marked by the + sign . For example, *girl* is + young, + human, + living, + countable . This indicates that the word *girl* has these four semantic features : young, human, living, and countable .

2. **Negative feature** or minus feature . It is marked by the – sign . For example, *woman* is – young; *dog*, – human; *book*, – living; *water*, – countable . This *minus* indicates *not*, i.e., the absence of the feature .

3. **Double feature** or plus-minus feature . It is marked by the ∓ signs . It indicates that the word can have both the positive and negative features . For example, *student* is ∓ masculine; it

can be used as masculine and as feminine . So are *teacher, nurse, doctor, driver, swimmer, child,* and *person* .

4. **Zero feature** . It is marked by the Ø sign . It indicates that a certain feature does not apply to a certain word . For example, *book* is Ø young, Ø masculine . This indicates that *book* cannot be described as + young nor as – young . Similarly, *book* cannot be described as + masculine nor as – masculine .

Relations between Semantic Features

Semantic features may show some relations of implication . For example, + human ⊐ + living : if it is + human, it is + living . This may be called **feature redundancy** or feature implication . More examples are :

1. + countable   ⊐ + concrete

2. + living   ⊐ + concrete

3. + male   ⊐ + masculine

4. + concrete   ⊐ – abstract

5. + masculine   ⊐ – feminine

6. + male   ⊐ – female

7. + young   ⊐ – adult

8. + human   ⊐ + living

9. + visible   ⊐ + concrete

Semantic Features and Synonymy

If we analyze each word of any synonymous pair into its semantic features, we shall discover that the two synonyms have the same set of semantic features . On the other hand, if we analyze two words each into its semantic features and find that they have the same semantic features, we conclude that the two words are synonyms .

In other words, synonymy can prove the sameness of semantic features, and the sameness of semantic features can prove synonymy . For example, *teacher* and *instructor* are + human, + noun, ∓ masculine, + living, + countable, + doer, + transitive, + teach, + job . The sameness of semantic features leads to the conclusion that the two words are synonymous . However, if we know that A and B are synonyms, then we can safely conclude that they do have the same semantic features .

With more detailed and careful analysis of the semantic features of two synonyms, we can determine whether their synonymy is complete or partial . For example, *profound* and *deep* are a case of partial synonymy because we can say *profound* or *deep thinking* and we can say *deep river,* but we cannot say **profound river* .

Semantic features and Antonymy

As we can prove or explain synonymy through semantic features, so we can use these features to prove or explain antonymy as well .

If we examine Table 7 - 1, we may notice the following :

Table 7 – 1 : Antonymy and Semantic Features

Word	living	human	male	young
boy	+	+	+	+
girl	+	+	–	+
man	+	+	+	–
woman	+	+	–	–

1. *Boy* has four positive semantic features, *girl* three positive and one negative, *man* three positive and one negative, and *woman* two positive and two negative .

2. The difference between *boy* and *girl* is one feature : + male, – male . So is the difference between *man* and *woman* . Thus, each pair is binary antonyms .

3. The difference between *boy* and *man* is ∓ young . So is the difference between *girl* and *woman* . This makes these pairs affinity antonyms .

4. The difference between *girl* and *man* is two features : gender and age . So is the case with *boy* and *woman* .

5. The difference between *boy* and *girl* is the same as that between *man* and *woman*, i.e., + male, – male . This proves that the difference in features determines the difference in meanings .

124

6. The relation of *boy* to *man* is like the relation of *girl* to *woman,* a difference in + young, – young .

7. The difference between *boy / woman* is larger than the difference between *boy / girl* : gender and age in the former, but gender only in the latter . The more uncommon the semantic features between two words are, the larger the meaning difference is going to be .

8. The difference between *girl / man* is larger than that between *girl / woman* : gender and age in the former, but age only in the latter . With more differences between features of words, their meanings become more and more different .

If A and B are antonyms, they should differ in one basic semantic feature at least . In addition, if two words (A and B) belonging to the same semantic field differ in one basic semantic feature or more, A and B must be antonyms .

Basic Semantic Features

Not all semantic features are equally significant . There are *distinctive features* or **basic features,** and there are non-distinctive or **secondary features** .

For example, the color of the *apple* is not a basic feature of *apple;* it can be green, yellow, or red, but still an *apple* . So is the size of the apple : it is not a basic feature . The *apple* can be large, medium, or small, yet it remains an *apple* .

Another example is the semantic features of *man* and *woman* . The eye color or the skin color is not a basic feature in the case of *man / woman* . Both the *man* and *woman* can have the same eye color and the same skin color, so these colors are not **distinctive features** of *man / woman* . Such features are called insignificant or **non-functional features** .

Rules of Semantic Features

Semantic features enable us to put words in equations like this :

$$1. \quad \frac{man}{woman} = \frac{boy}{girl} = \frac{+\,\text{male}}{-\,\text{male}}$$

This means that the distinctive feature between *man / woman* and *boy / girl* is + male / − male .

2. From equation (1), we can easily derive this equation :

$$\frac{woman}{man} = \frac{girl}{boy} = \frac{-\,\text{male}}{+\,\text{male}}$$

3. From equation (1), we can also derive this equation :

$$\frac{man}{boy} = \frac{woman}{girl} = \frac{-\,\text{young}}{+\,\text{young}}$$

$$boy \qquad girl \qquad +\,\text{young}$$

$$or \; \frac{}{man} = \frac{}{woman} = \frac{}{-\,young}$$

The previous discussion can, in fact, give us five semantic rules :

1. If the two words A and B have the same semantic features, A and B are synonyms .

2. If A and B are synonyms, they have the same semantic features .

3. If A and B belong to the same semantic field and differ in one basic semantic feature or more, A and B are anytonyms .

4. If A and B are antonyms, they must differ in one basic semantic feature or more .

5. The more two words differ in semantic features, the more they differ in meaning .

Measurement of Meaning

Despite the fact that meaning is primarily abstract, it is measurable . Meaning can be measured through three ways : association, scaled oppositeness, and gradation .

Measurement by **association** requires stimulating respondents to remember the first word that comes to the mind as a reaction to the measured word . For example, if we want to analyze the word *weep,* we ask hundreds of people about the first word they spontaneously associate with *weep* upon hearing the word . Such associations would most probably be words like *baby, woman, tears, eye, sadness,* and *joy* . These associations will be used as semantic features or components of the meaning of *weep* .

As for measurement by **scaled oppositeness,** this can be done through a seven-option scale with two opposites on each end . This scale, as in Table 7 – 2, is given to scores or hundreds of respondents to mark their choices .

Table 7 – 2 : Meaning-Measurement Scale

Teacher	to a maximal extent	to a great extent	to some extent	neither this nor that	to some extent	to a great extent	to a maximal extent	Teacher
merciful			X					cruel
fair		X						unfair
encouraging			X					discouraging
knowledgeable		X						ignorant

This table, Table 7 – 2, uses opposites on both sides, with three levels for each feature, whether positive or negative, and a neutral level in between . Responses are counted, and the frequency of each option is specified . Accordingly, related semantic features, here of the word *teacher,* are determined .

The third way of measuring meaning is **gradation** . Here, respondents are required to grade up or down a group of related words . For example, grade this group : *warm, hot, rather hot,*

128

very hot, boiling hot .Another example is *rather cold, very cold, cold, chilly, icy-cold, freezing cold* .

EXERCISES

Exercise 7 - 1

Are these statements true (T) or false (F) ?

1. Every word has a form, meaning, and distribution .

2. A word has a spoken form and a visible form .

3. The written form of the word is its visible form .

4. Both the written form and spoken form consist of phones .

5. Word distribution is two types : grammatical and stylistic .

6. The grammatical distribution of a word usually determines its function in the sentence .

7. The stylistic distribution of a word determines the situation in which it is to be used .

8. The grammatical distribution of a word differs from its meaning and has no relation with it .

9. That a word is a noun, for example, is part of its stylistic distribution .

10. That a word is used in poetry and not in prose is part of its stylistic distribution .

11. The most questionable part of a word is its form, not its meaning or distribution .

12. The words *boy, girl, child,* and *man* have one
feature in common, i.e., + human .   _____

Exercise 7 - 2

Give one common semantic feature for each group .

1. horse, ram, lion, fish .   _____

2. chair, door, window, car .   _____

3. doctor, engineer, lawyer, teacher .   _____

4. lady, girl, woman, widow .   _____

5. brother, sister, uncle, aunt .   _____

Exercise 7 - 3

**What is the distinctive feature of each pair ? Example : +
male, – male .**

1. he-student, she-student   _____

2. colt, filly   _____

3. bull, cow   _____

4. boy, man   _____

5. brother, sister   _____

6. uncle, aunt   _____

7. son, daughter   _____

8. girl, woman   _____

9. grandfather, grandmother   _____

10. father, grandfather   _____

11. son, father   _____

12. son, grandson   _____

13. grandson, granddaughter _____

Exercise 7 - 4

Fill in the blank with the proper word that makes the equation correct .

1. $\dfrac{\text{son}}{\text{daughter}} = \dfrac{\text{grandson}}{?}$

2. $\dfrac{\text{daughter}}{\text{son}} = \dfrac{\text{sister}}{?}$

3. $\dfrac{\text{paternal uncle}}{\text{paternal aunt}} = \dfrac{\text{maternal uncle}}{?}$

4. $\dfrac{\text{paternal uncle}}{\text{maternal uncle}} = \dfrac{\text{paternal aunt}}{?}$

Exercise 7 - 5

Refer back to the previous exercise, and mention the distinctive feature of every equation .

1. _____

2. _____

3. _____

4. _____

Exercise 7 - 6

What do these feature symbols stand for ?

1. +   _____

2. —   _____

3. ∓   _____

4. Ø   _____

CHAPTER 8

SEMANTIC FIELDS

Every language has hundreds of thousands of different words . English has about one million words, for example . In fact, the number of words in a language depends on how words are counted : Are the words *write, wrote, written, writing, writes,* and *writer* considered as one word (with six different derivations) or six different words ? Despite this huge number of words, the words of English or any other language are not non-classifiable; they can be grouped and classified depending on their meaning into different semantic fields .

Nature of the Semantic Field

What is a semantic field ? For example, the words *nose, eye, ear, mouth, tongue, head, heart, brain,* and many others belong to one semantic field that may be called *body organs* . The words *cat, dog, cow, goat, wolf, fox, lion,* and *tiger* belong to a semantic field called *animals* .The words *car, lorry, truck, bus,* and *microbus* belong to a semantic field called *transportation means* .

Semantic fields are the output of many processes of classification and sub-classification . The farther the classification goes, the more fields we have . The more fields we have, the narrower each field becomes . The field of *animals* contains thousands of members . The field of *birds*, a sub-class of *animals*, contains less members than the field of *animals* . The field of *sea-birds*, a sub-class of *birds*, contains less members than the field of *birds*, and so on . The narrower a field is, the less members it has . The semantic field is a group of words closely related in their meaning .

Members of the Semantic Field

The semantic field contains a group of related words . What words can be members in one semantic field ?

1. Synonyms usually come under the same semantic field .

2. Derivatives from the same root usually belong to the same field, e.g., *phone, phoneme, allophone, phonetic, phonemic, phonic, phonetics, phonemics, phonetically, phonemically, phonetician* .

3. Hyponyms and superordinates belong to the same semantic field, e.g., *cat / animal, apple / fruit, boy / human, brother / relative* .

4. Antonyms, regardless of their type, belong to the same semantic field, e.g., *male / female, sell / buy, north / south, east / south, Saturday / Sunday, orange / banana / apple, room / house* .

5. Associated words may belong to the same semantic field .
Look at these examples :

a. the murmer of water

b. the roar of lions

c. children's innocence

d. The ear hears .

e. The eye sees .

f. The heart beats .

g. The stomach digests .

h. belief in God

i. belief in the Last Day

These examples show four types of **horizontal association** : *of*-structures, possessive structures, subject-verb structures, and noun-prepositional-phrase structures .

Multiple Membership

A word may be a member in more than one semantic field . For example, the word *ear* may be a member in these fields : *body oragns, head organs,* and *the hearing system* . The word *whale* may be a member in these fields : *living creatures, animals,* and *sea animals* . The word *pen* can belong to these fields : *writing* and *stationery* .

In fact, most words belong to more than one semantic field, a phenomenon called **multiple membership** of words . This may cause some overlap between different fields . However, a word cannot usually belong to equally ranking fields; it can belong to fields of different ranks in the hierarchy .

Examples of Semantic Fields

Any group of words that may come under one title or one type can form a semantic field . However, the number of fields is questionable, and, consequently, the broadness of the field is controversial .

For example, one can have one semantic field for all animals, called the field of *animals* . However, this field may be divided into narrower sub-fields such as *mammals, birds, reptiles, birds,* and *insects* . Each of these **sub-fields** can be divided further into narrower fields . *Insects,* for instance, can be divided into these fields : *useful insects, harmful insects, flying insects,* and *non-flying insects* .

Here are some examples of possible semantic fields to which different words may belong : relatives, mammals, birds, sea-animals, reptiles, insects, flowers, herbs, fruitful trees, forest trees, medicines, diseases, kitchen utensils, furniture, transportation means, body organs, war equipment, civil jobs, military ranks, colors, printed materials, stationery, sports, banking, administration, commerce, vocations, professions, etc . The complete list is very much longer than this one, and each field can, of course, be classified into many narrower sub-fields .

Words and Semantic Fields

If you want to distribute different words under different semantic fields, you have to follow these steps :

1. Specify the **major semantic fields** as the first step, e.g., *humans, animals, plants*, etc .

2. Branch the major fields into **minor sub-fields** . For example, *humans* is branched into *male* and *female*, and each into *adult* and *non-adult* . Another example is *relatives*, branched into *paternal* and *maternal*, each of which is branched into *male* and *female* . A third example is *diseases*, branched into diseases of the digestive system, respiratory system, nervous system, blood circulation system, etc .

3. Distribute the words directly under the minor sub-fields, not under the major fields .

Notice that every word must come under a certain minor sub-field . If a word fails to belong to any field, this indicates that the available fields are inadequate, and such fields have to be re-adjusted . Accordingly, each word is made to belong to one minor sub-field only . A word can have multiple membership in a major field and a minor one, e.g., *cat* as a member in *animals* and *domestic animals*, but it cannot be a member in two major fields or two minor fields of equal rank .

Types of Semantic Fields

Look at these groups of words :

1. *book, copybook, chair, car, room, tree, mountain, sea, river, plane, bird, fish, iron .*
2. *walk, run, sit, stand, write, swim, sleep, study, read .*
3. *walking, translation, dictation, greatness, sleeping, reading, tolerance .*
4. *far, near, clever, generous, red, happy, tolerant, easy, difficult .*
5. *in, on, at, to, over, between, and, or .*

If we examine these five groups, we find that Group 1 can be classified as **concrete beings** . Group 2 is **actions** in the language of semantics, i.e., verbs in the language of grammar . Group 3 is **abstracts** in semantics and abstract nouns in grammar . Group 4 is **qualities** in semantics and adjectives in grammar . Group 5 is **linkers** in semantics and particles in grammar .

These five domains are far from being final or uncontroversial . For example, why is *translate* an action and *translation* is not ? Why is *happiness* an abstract word and *happy* is not ?

Relations within the Semantic Field

As said before, it is not the case that all words or any words can belong to one semantic field . Only a selected group of words can belong to the same field .

Of course, synonyms belong to the same field owing to their sameness in sense and meaning . Hyponyms and their superordinates belong to the same field due to the strong semantic relation between both : the hyponym is a type of the superordinate, e.g., *cat / animal*,

Similarly, all types of antonyms belong to the same field . This includes all the nine types of antonyms : binary antonyms, gradable antonyms, converse antonyms, perpendicular antonyms, extensional antonyms, cyclic antonyms, rank antonyms, affinity antonyms, and partial antonyms .

All words that show sense similarity or sense dissimilarity should belong to the same semantic field . Remember that semantic fields include words only . Therefore, paraphrases, entailments, and contradictories do not and cannot belong to any semantic field because they are sentences, not words .

Applications of Semantic Fields

The semantic-field theory can be helpful in several ways, both theoretically and practically :

1. Semantic fields can offer an obvious help in revealing relations between word senses, i.e., synonymy, hyponymy, and antonymy, because these relations are basically relations between words belonging to the same semantic field .

2. The normal dictionary gives us a list of words ordered alphabetically, not semantically . The alphabetical order in the dictionary has the advantage of easy order and easy retrieval . On the other hand, we can imagine designing dictionaries based on semantic fields and ordered alphabetically at the same time . Thus, we benefit from both systems .

3. Classifying words according to semantic fields makes **contrastive analysis** of languages both easier and more comprehensive . Thus, we can know where two languages are different and where they are similar, semantically speaking .

4. Semantic fields give us a comprehensive picture about the nature of language and its words, instead of the dictionary list of thousands of words ordered alphabetically with no regard to sense or meaning . Those semantic fields show the semantic relations between words because such fields mainly depend on classification and grouping based on reference, sense, and meaning .

EXERCISES

Exercise 8 - 1

Decide whether each statement is true (T) or false (F) .

1. The semantic field is the same as extension . ...

2. The wider the semantic field, the more members it has . ...

3. The number of semantic fields in a language is not a controversial matter . _____

4. The semantic field is a group of unrelated words . _____

5. The semantic field includes words indicating concrete beings only . _____

6. Antonyms do not come under the same semantic field . _____

7. A word and its derivatives do not belong to the same semantic field . _____

8. The hyponym and the superordinate come under the same semantic field (SF) . _____

9. The words *student* and *students* come under the same SF . _____

10. Words in synonymy, hyponymy, or antonymy can replace one another vertically in a sentence; they are vertically related . _____

11. If words are not vertically related, they cannot belong to the same SF . _____

12. The words *eye* and *see* do not belong to the same SF . _____

13. Perpendicular antonymy does not allow words to be in the same SF . _____

14. Words in affinity antonymy cannot belong to the same SF . _____

15. Words in partial antonymy are in the same SF . _____

16. If a word belongs to a minor SF, it cannot belong to
    another minor SF .   _____

17. If a word belongs to a minor SF, it cannot belong to
    a major SF .   _____

18. Some words do not belong to any SF .   _____

19. Particles like prepositions and conjunctions do not
    belong to any SF .   _____

Exercise 8 - 2

**What is the type of each group : concrete beings (CB),
actions (AC), abstracts (AB), qualities (Q), or linkers (L) ?**

1. *lion, tiger, book, building*   _____

2. *on, in, from, to*   _____

3. *tourism, swimming, confusion, running*   _____

4. *continue, smile, climb, move*   _____

5. *large, small, old, new*   _____

Exercise 8 - 3

Suggest a suitable semantic field for each group .

1. *bed, chair, table, desk*   _____

2. *pen, pencil, eraser, paper*   _____

3. *car, lorry, truck, tanker*   _____

4. *oxygen, hydrogen, nitrogen, helium*   _____

5. *cucumber, lettuce, cabbage, cornflower*   _____

6. *school, college, university, kindergarten*   _____

7. *brother, sister, uncle, aunt*   _____

8. *blue, red, yellow, green*   _____

9. *headache, cold, ulcer, measles* ....

10. *magazine, newspaper, book, encyclopedia* ....

11. *east, west, south, north* ....

12. *father, mother, son, daughter* ....

Exercise 8 - 4

Underline the word that does not belong to the group, and suggest a suitable semantic field for the group .

1. *banana, apple, orange, apricot, flower* ....
2. *uncle, aunt, friend, grandmother, cousin* ....
3. *car, ship, plane, lake, boat* ....
4. *honesty, generosity, truthfulness, reliability, largeness* ....
5. *second, minute, court, hour, day* ....
6. *running, walking, thinking, jumping, skating* ....

Exercise 8 - 5

What is the proper semantic field of each group ?

1. *prayer, fasting, pilgrimage, charity* ....
2. *force, momentum, gravity, acceleration* ....
3. *equation, progression, addition, subtraction* ....
4. *triangle, perpendicular, rectangle, square* ....
5. *phoneme, allophone, labial, nasal* ....
6. *synonymy, antonymy, hyponymy, polysemy* ....
7. *motive, stimulus, response, instinct* ....
8. *root, stem, leaf, fruit* ....
9. *bile, stomach, brain, heart* ....
10. *interaction, formula, acid, hydrogen* ....

CHAPTER 9

MEANING AND LOGIC

Semantics deals with the word meaning and sentence meaning, whereas logic deals with reasoning principles . Of course, reasoning principles depend heavily on meaning . Thus semantics and logic are strongly related . In this chapter, we shall see how meaning and logic are related .

Logical Words

In every language there are words or expressions that cannot be RE's or PE's . Words like *London, John,* and *Hani* can be RE's . Words like *student, man,* and *honest* can be PE's which can be used to inform about RE's, e.g., *Hani is an honest man* . However, words like *and, or, but, if, all, some,* and *not* cannot be RE's or PE's . They are called **linking words** or logical words .

The Logic of *And*

Look at these S's :

1. Hani came . (A)

2. Ali came . (B)

3. Hani came and Ali came .

4. Ali came and Hani came .

For S_3 to be true, both S_1 and S_2 must be true . If either S_1 or S_2 is false, this makes S_3 false . The truth of S_3 requires the truth of both S_1 and S_2 . If S_1 only is true or S_2 only is true, this makes S_3 false .

Let us assume that S_1 is true and S_2 is true; it follows that S_3 is true . Let us see S_3 as made of two components A *and* B, i.e., A & B, where *and* is symbolized as & . It follows that *A & B* is true . If *A & B* is true, *B & A* is true . We can call this rule the **rule of *and* commutativity :**

A & B true	(premise)
B & A true	(conclusion)

Inference from *And*

Look at these S`s :

1. Hani passed the test . (A)

2. Ali passed the test . (B)

3. Hani passed the test and Ali passed the test .

4. Hani and Ali passed the test .

We can use *and* to combine S_1 and S_2 into S_3 . By omitting common words, we can condense S_3 into S_4 .

145

If S$_1$ is true and S$_2$ is true, S$_4$ is necessarily true, so is S$_3$. Thus, S$_4$ requires two true premises .

A true   (premise 1)
B true   (premise 2)

A & B true   (conclusion)

If *A & B* is true, then A is true . Similarly, if *A & B* is true, B is true .

Thus, we have four rules related to *and* :
1. If A is true and B is true, *A & B* is true .
2. If *A & B* is true, *B & A* is true .
3. If *A & B* is true, A is true .
4. If *A & B* is true, B is true .

Truth Probabilities of *And*

When *and* is used to combine two S's like A and B, there are four truth probabilities :
1. Both A and B are true .
2. A is true, and B is false .
3. A is false, and B is true .
4. Both A and B are false .

If both A and B are true, then the compound sentence (CS) is true . If A is true and B is false, then the CS is false . If A is false and B is true, then the CS is false . If both A and B are

146

false, the CS is false . Table 9 – 1 shows these four probabilities as such :

1. A true   (premise 1)
    B true   (premise 2)
    _____
    A & B true   (conclusion)

2. A true   (premise 1)
    B false   (premise 2)
    _____
    A & B false   (conclusion)

3. A false   (premise 1)
    B true   (premise 2)
    _____
    A & B false   (conclusion)

4. A false   (premise 1)
    B false   (premise 2)
    _____
    A & B false   (conclusion)

Table 9 - 1 : Truth Probabilities of *And*

Probability No.	First Premise (A)	Second Premise (B)	Conclusion (A & B)
1	T	T	T
2	T	F	F
3	F	T	F
4	F	F	F

The Logic of *Or*

Most probably all languages have a conjunction like *or*, which means *option*, symbolized here as v . Look at these sentences :

1. Hani has come or Ali has left . (A or B)

2. Ali has left or Hani has come . (B or A)

Logically, S₁ can be phrased as *A v B*, and S₂ can be phrased as *B v A* . For S₁ to be true, there are three probabilities :

a. A is true, and B is false .

b. A is false, and B is true .

c. Both A and B are true .

Thus, the truth of *A v B* is secured by the truth of either A or B or the truth of both . As for the falsity of *A v B*, it occurs only if both A and B are false.

Notice that commutativity applies also to *or* sentences as it applies to *and* sentences . If *A v B* is true, so is *B v A* . Back to S₁ and S₂ if S₁ is true, then S₂ is true . Notice that S₁ is *A v B* and S₂ is *B v A* . We can call this rule the **rule of *or* commutativity** .

If *A v B* is true, this does not necessarily mean that A is true and B is true . The truth of one of them is enough to make *A v B* true .

If *and* and *or* come in one sentence, the sentence may become ambiguous, e.g., *He left for Rome and he met her or he visited them* (A & B v C) . Does *or* make the option between A B and C or the option between B and C ? Does *and* combine A and B or combine A on one side and B v C on the other side ?

Truth Probabilities of *Or*

Let us see the probabilities of *or* sentences concerning truth and falsity . We have to assume that each *or* sentence must have two components A and B linked by *or,* e.g., *He flew to Athens (A) or he sailed to Rome (B)* . The probabilities here are these four :

1. A is true; B is true .

2. A is true; B is false .

3. A is false; B is true .

4. A is false; B is false .

Each previous probability leads to a certain logical inference :

1. If A is true and B is true, the compound sentence (CS) is true .

```
A  true      ( premise 1 )
B  true      ( premise 2 )
─────────────
A v B true   ( conclusion )
```

2. If A is true and B is false, the CS is true .

```
A  true      ( premise 1 )
B  false     ( premise 2 )
─────────────
A v B  true   ( conclusion )
```

3. If A is false and B is true, then the CS is true .

> A false   (premise 1)
> B true   (premise 2)
> _____
> A v B true   (conclusion)

4. If both A and B are false, then the CS is false .

> A false   (premise 1)
> B false   (premise 2)
> _____
> A v B false   (conclusion)

This table (Table 9 – 2) summarizes the four probabilities of *or* sentences . T stands for *true* and F for *false* .

Table 9 – 2 : Truth Probabilities of *Or*

Probability No.	First Premise (A)	Second Premise (B)	Conclusion (A v B)
1	T	T	T
2	T	F	T
3	F	T	T
4	F	F	F

The Logic of *But*

Most languages, if not all, have *but* as a logical word linking two S's into a compound sentence (CS), e.g., *John has left (A), but Edward has arrived (B)* . For this CS, there are four probabilities concerning truth and falsity :

150

1. If A is true and B is true, then the CS is true .

> A true   (premise 1)
> B true   (premise 2)
> _____
> A but B true   (conclusion)

2. If A is true and B is false, then the CS is false .

> A true   (premise 1)
> B false   (premise 2)
> _____
> A but B false   (conclusion)

3. If A is false and B is true, then the CS is false .

> A false   (premise 1)
> B true   (premise 2)
> _____
> A but B false   (conclusion)

4. If A is false and B is false, then the CS is false .

> A false   (premise 1)
> B false   (premise 2)
> _____
> A but B false   (conclusion)

This shows that for *A but B* to be true, both A and B must be true . If either A or B is false, then *A but B* is false . This makes the truth probabilities of *but* identical with those of *and* . *A and B* is true only if both A and B are true . Similarly, *A but B* is true only if both A and B are true . The falsity of A or B makes *A & B* false and also makes *A but B* false . Table 9 – 3 summarizes the truth probabilities of *but*, where T stands for *true* and F for *false* .

Table 9 – 3 : Truth Probabilities of *But*

Probability No.	First Premise (A)	Second Premise (B)	Conclusion (A but B)
1	T	T	T
2	T	F	F
3	F	T	F
4	F	F	F

The Logic of Negators

All languages have negation, negative sentences, and negators, i.e., particles that negate, e.g., *not, never, no* . Negators are considered **logical words;** so are *and, or,* and *but* . In logic, negation is symbolized as ~ .

Look at these S's :
1. *John swam yesterday .*
2. *~ (John swam yesterday) .*
3. *John has left and Ali has arrived .*
4. *~ (John has left) and ~ (Ali has arrived) .*
5. *A*
6. *~ A*
7. *A & B*
8. *~ A & ~ B*

If we examine the previous eight sentences, we notice that S_2 is the negation of S_1 and S_4 is the negation of S_3 . Notice that S_4 needs two negators because it has two combined

152

statements . In addition, S_6 is the negation of S_5, and S_8 is the negation of S_7 .

Truth Probabilities of Negators

If A is true, the negation of A is false . Moreover, if A is false, its negation is true . If A is true, the negation of its negation will be true . If A is false, the negation of its negation will be false .

If we use symbols, we have these four probabilities :

1. A true (premise 1)
   _____
   ~ A false (conclusion)

2. A false (premise 1)
   _____
   ~ A true (conclusion)

3. A true (premise 1)
   _____
   ~ ~ A true (conclusion)

4. A false (premise 1)
   _____
   ~ ~ A false (conclusion)

In other words, if we negate a true S, the output will be false . If we negate a false S, the output will be true . If we negate the negative of a true S, the output will be true . If we negate the negative of a false S, the output will be false .

153

The Logic of *If*

All languages have a conditional word like *if*, which is another logical word like *and, or,* and *but* .

Look at these sentences :
1. *If he comes, she will leave .*
2. *She will leave if he comes .*
3. *He comes* → *she leaves .*

In normal language, the *if*-clause can initiate the sentence as in S_1 or can come at the end as in S_2 . However, in logical phrasing, the condition appears first, followed by the symbol → , which stands for *the condition of,* and the result of the condition comes after the symbol, as in S_3 .

As for the relation between the condition and its result, there are two possible logical inferences :

1. If A is the condition and B is the result and if A is true, i.e., is realized, B is true or realized .

A → B   (premise 1)
A realized   (premise 2)
_____
B realized   (conclusion)

2. If A is the condition and B is the result and if B is not realized, A is also not realized .

A → B   (premise 1)
~ B   (premise 2)
_____
~ A   (conclusion)

Applying these two logical inferences to *If you study, you will pass*, this means that if studying is realized, passing will be realized . If passing is not realized, this means that studying has not been realized .

EXERCISES

Exercise 9 -1

What symbol in logic stands for each of the following ?

1. and _____

2. or _____

3. negation _____

4. negation of

negation _____

5. condition of _____

Exercise 9 - 2

Fill in each blank with true (T) or false (F) .

1. If (C & D) is true and C is true, then D is _____ .

2. If C is true and D is true, then (C & D) is _____ .

3. If C is true and D is false, then (C v D) is _____ .

4. If C is true and D is false, then (C but D) is _____ .

5. If C is false and D is false, then (C but D) is _____ .

6. If C is true, then ~ C is _____ .

7. If C is false, then ~ ~ C is _____ .

8. If C is true, then ~ ~ C is _____ .

Exercise 9 - 3

Decide whether each is true (T) or false (F) .

1. The truth probabilities of *and* are narrower than those of *or* . ...

2. The truth probabilities of *and* and *but* are identical . _____

3. The truth of (*A* & *B*) requires the truth of both components . _____

4. If a component of (*A* & *B*) is false, the CS is false . _____

5. The truth of the *or* sentence requires the truth of both components . ...

6. The truth of the *or* sentence requires the truth of one component only . ...

7. The falsity of one component of the *or* sentence results in the sentence falsity . _____

8. The *or* sentence is false only if both components are false . ...

9. The *but* sentence is true only if both components are true . _____

10. The truth probabilities of *but* and *and* are identical . ...

11. The truth probabilities of *and* and *or* are the same . _____

12. The *but* sentence is false if both components are false . _____

13. The *but* sentence is false only if both components are false . _____

14. If either component of the *but* sentence is false, the S is false . _____

15. The *but* S is true only if both components are true . _____

156

16. Negating a true S gives a false S .   ·········

17. Negating a false S gives a false S .   ——

18. If we negate a true S twice, we get a true S .   ——

19. If we negate a false S twice, we get a true S .   ·········

20. If A is the condition of B and A is realized, B is realized .   ——

Answers to the Exercises

Chapter 1

Exercise 1 - 1

1. meaning
2. linguistics
3. referent
4. oral, written
5. mind, world
6. information, social
7. sentence, speaker's, hearer's

Exercise 1 - 2

1. T	2. T	3. F	4. F	5. F	6. F
7. F	8. F	9. T	10. F	11. F	12. T

Exercise 1 - 3

1. The sun is larger than the earth .
2. * The earth are larger than the sun .
3. * The sun larger than the earth .
4. The earth is larger than the sun .

Exercise 1 - 4

1. – – +
2. – + +
3. + + +
4. – – +
5. – + +
6. + + –

Exercise 1 - 5

| 1. F | 2. F | 3. T | 4. F | 5. F | 6. F |
| 7. F | 8. T | 9. F | 10. T | 11. T | |

Exercise 1 - 6

| 1. NC | 2. C | 3. C | 4. NC | 5. C | 6. NC |

Chapter 2

Exercise 2 - 1

| 1. RE | 2. RE | 3. PE | 4. PE |
| 5. PE | 6. linking | 7. both | 8. linking |

Exercise 2 - 2

| 1. lies on | 2. ate | 3. red | 4. in |

Exercise 2 - 3

| 1. he | 2. Khalid | 3. you, Ali | 4. — |

Exercise 2 - 4

| 1. skilled, doctor | 2. brilliant, leader |
| 3. better, in, swimming | 4. planes, similar, birds |

Exercise 2 - 5

| 1. Yes | 2. Yes | 3. No | 4. No |

Exercise 2 - 6

1. three   2. one   3. one   4. two   5. two

Exercise 2 - 7

1. RE   2. predicate   3. predicate   4. predicate   5. predicate

Exercise 2 - 8

1. G   2. NG   3. G   4. NG   5. G

Exercise 2 - 9

1. I, you, this   2. we, here
3. there, now   4. go, today, tomorrow

Exercise 2 - 10

1. F   2. T   3. F   4. F   5. T
6. F   7. T   8. F   9. T   10. T

Chapter 3

Exercise 3 - 1

1. F   2. F   3. T   4. T   5. F
6. F   7. F   8. T   9. T   10. T

Exercise 3 – 2

1. assist   2. displeased   3. sad   4. pleased
5. tip   6. back   7. positive   8. teach

Exercise 3 - 3

1. P   2. P   3. P   4. NP   5. P

Exercise 3 - 4

1. T   2. T   3. T   4. S

Exercise 3 - 5

1. $=$ 2. $\equiv$ 3. $\supset$ 4. $\rightarrow$

Exercise 3 - 6

1. F   2. F   3. T   4. T   5. T   6. T   7. T
8. F   9 F   10. F   11. T   12. T   13. T   14. T

Exercise 3 - 7

1. H   2. Su   3. Su   4. H
5. S   6. S   7. S

Exercise 3 - 8

1. P   2. E   3. P   4. P   5. P   6. E

Exercise 3 - 9

1. F   2. S   3. S

Exercise 3 - 10

1. paraphrase   2. words   3. sentences

4. mutual   5. entailment   6. hyponymy

7. entailment   8. hyponymy, entailment   9. paraphrase, entailment

10. superordinate   11. synonymous   12. paraphrase

13. hyponym, superordinate

Chapter 4

Exercise 4 - 1

1. G	2. G	3. B	4. B	5. B
6. G	7. B	8. B	9. G	10. B

Exercise 4 - 2

1. C   2. G   3. C   4. C   5. C   6. B   7. B   8. G

Exercise 4 - 3

1. D   2. ND   3. ND   4. D   5. ND   6. D   7. ND   8. ND

Exercise 4 - 4

1. E   2. E   3. E   4. P   5. E   6. P   7. E   8. P

Exercise 4 - 5

1. C   2. A   3. C   4. C   5. R   6. A   7. A   8. R

Exercise 4 - 6

1. B   2. M   3. B   4. M   5. B   6. B   7. M   8. B

Exercise 4 - 7

1. gradable   2. extensional   3. rank
4. binary   5. partial   6. cyclic
7. perpendicular 8. affinity   9. converse

Exercise 4 - 8

1. F	2. T	3. T	4. F	5. T
6. T	7. F	8. T	9. F	10. F

Exercise 4 - 9

1. wrong	2. allow	3. six	4. falsity
5. distrust	6. continue	7. follow	8. displeased
9. backward	10. extravagance		

(Many other answers are possible .)

Exercise 4 - 10

1. multiple	2. senses	3. sentences	4. non-directional
5. gradable	6. extensional	7. rank	8. antonymy

Chapter 5

Exercise 5 - 1

1. A	2. A	3. A	4. A	5. A	6. U
7. A	8. A	9. A	10. A	11. U	12. U

Exercise 5 - 2

See the dictionary if necessary .

Exercise 5 - 3

1. H	2. P	3. P	4. P	5. P
6. H	7. H	8. H	9. P	10. H

Exercise 5 - 4

1. A, LA   2. A, LA   3. N, –   4. A, LA   5. A, GA
6. A, GA   7. A, GA   8. A, LA   9. N, –   10. A, GA

Exercise 5 - 5

1. a. Parents offer help .   b. Parents need help .
2. a. Only fruit is dry .   b. Both fruit and vegetable are dry .
3. a. Only books are modern.   b. Both books and novels are modern .
4. a. To visit patients . . .   b. Patients who visit . . .
5. a. He hit with the stick .   b. The thief had a stick .

Exercise 5 - 6

1. possessive structure   2. *and* structure
3. *and* structure   4. *–ing* structure
5. the prepositional phrase structure

Chapter 6

Exercise 6 - 1

1. S   2. A   3. A   4. A   5. S   6. C

Exercise 6 - 2

1. T   2. F   3. T   4. T   5. T   6. F
7. F   8. T   9. F   10. F   11. T

Exercise 6 - 3

1. autumn, falling   2. languages, the organ of speech .

3. meaning, one of the five senses   4. water source, a season, etc .

Exercise 6 - 4

1. body movements   2. facial feelings   3. tone

4. conversers' roles   5. previous relationship   6. environment

Exercise 6 - 5

1. large, small   2. tall   3. few   4. warm

Exercise 6 - 6

1. . . .

2. a word that joins two words of the same part of speech

3. . . .

4. the day after Monday and before Wednesday

5. brave

6. poor

7. a kind of fruit

Exercise 6 - 7

1. F   2. T   3. F   4. F

Exercise 6 - 8

1. love   2. generosity

3. support   4. bravery, sacrifice

Exercise 6 - 9

1. murmur   2. puff   3. crush   4. squeak

Exercise 6 - 10

1. sentence   2. word   3. phrase   4. morpheme

Exercise 6 - 11

1. recipient   2. instrument   3. agent
4. result   5. time   6. goal

Chapter 7

Exercise 7 - 1

1. T   2. T   3. T   4. F   5. T   6. T
7. T   8. F   9. F   10. T   11. F   12. T

Exercise 7 - 2

1. + animal   2.   −   3. + human   4. − male   5. + relative
              living

Exercise 7 – 3

1. + male, − male   2. + male, − male
3. + male, − male   4. + young, − young
5. + male, − male   6. + male, − male
7. + male, − male   8. + young, − young
9. + male, − male   10. + 1G, + 2G (where G stands for generation)
11. − 1G, + 1G   12. − 1G, − 2G
13. + male, − male

Exercise 7 - 4

1. granddaughter   2. brother
3. maternal aunt   4. maternal aunt

Exercise 7 - 5

1. + male / – male
2. – male / + male
3. + male / – male
4. + father-related /
   + mother-related

Exercise 7 - 6

1. positive feature
2. negative feature
3. double feature
4. zero feature

Chapter 8

Exercise 8 - 1

1. F	2. T	3. F	4. F	5. F
6. F	7. F	8. T	9. T	10. T
11. F	12. F	13. F	14. F	15. T
16. T	17. F	18. F	19. F	

Exercise 8 - 2

1. CB	2. L	3. AB	4. AC	5. Q

Exercise 8 - 3

1. furniture
2. stationery
3. means of transportation
4. gases
5. vegetables
6. educational institutions
7. relatives
8. colors
9. illness
10. printed materials
11. directions
12. family members

Exercise 8 - 4

1. flower, fruit

2. friend, relatives

3. lake, means of transport

4. – , virtues

5. court, time units

6. thinking, sports

Exercise 8 - 5

Different answers are possible here .

1. religion

2. physics or dynamics

3. mathematics

4. geometry

5. phonetics

6. semantics

7. psychology

8. botany

9. body organs

10. chemistry

Chapter 9

Exercise 9 - 1

1. &   2. v   3. ~   4. ~ ~   5. →

Exercise 9 - 2

1. T   2. T   3. T   4. F   5. F   6. F   7. F   8. T

Exercise 9 -3

1. T	2. T	3. T	4. T	5. F
6. T	7. F	8. T	9. T	10. T
11. F	12. T	13. T	14. T	15. T
16. T	17. F	18. T	19. F	20. T

Selected Bibliography

Alston, W. P. *Philosophy of Language* . Englewood Cliffs, N. J. : Prentice-Hall, 1994 .

Bach, E. & Harms, R. T. (eds.) *Universals in Linguistic Theory* . New York : Holt Rinehart, 1998 .

Bendix, E. M. *Componential Analysis of General Vocabulary* . The Hague : Mouton, 2004 .

Berlin, B. & Kay, P. *Basic Color Terms : Their Universality and Evolution* . Berkeley : University of California Press, 2005 .

Black, M. *Models and Metaphors : Studies in Language and Philosophy* . Ithaca, NY : Cornell University Press, 2002 .

Brooke-Rose, C. *A Grammar of Metaphor* . London : Secker & Warburg, 2001 .

Carnap, R. *Introduction to Semantics* . Cambridge, MA : Harvard University Press, 2002 .

————— . *Meaning and Necessity* . Chicago IL : University of Chicago Press , 2003 .

Clark, H. H. & Clark, E. V. *Psychology and Language : An Introduction to Psycholinguistics* . New York : Harcourt Brace Jovanovich, 2001 .

Cole, P. & Morgan, J. L. (eds.) *Syntax and Semantics, Vol.* 3. New York : Academic Press, 2004 .

Cole, P. & Sadock, J. M. (eds.) *Syntax and Semantics, Vol.* 8. New York : Academic Press, 2001 .

Davidson, D. & Harman, G, (eds.) *Semantics of Natural Language* . Dordrecht : Rerdel, 2003 .

Fodor, J. A. *Psychosemantics* .Cambridge, MA : MIT Press, 2004 .

Geach, P. *Reference and Generality* .Ithaca, NY : Cornell University Press, 2005 .

Gruber, J. S. *Lexical Structures in Syntax and Semantics* .Amsterdam : North Holland, 2005 .

Kempson, R. *Semantic Theory* . Cambridge : Cambridge University Press, 2001 .

Kimball, J. (ed.) *Syntax and Semantics, Vol.* 4. New York and London : Academic Press, 2004 .

Leech, G. N. *Principles of Pragmatics* . London : Longman, 2003.

Leech, G. N. *Semantics,* 2nd edition . Harmondsworth : Penguin Books, 2002 .

Levin, S. R. *The Semantics of Metaphor* . Baltimore and London : The Johns Hopkins University Press, 2001 .

Levinson, S . *Pragmatics* . Cambridge : Cambridge University Press, 2004 .

Loar, B. *Mind and Meaning* . Cambridge : Cambridge University Press, 2006 .

Lyons, J. *Language, Meaning, and Context* . London : Fontana, 2005 .

————— . *Semantics* (2 volumes) . Cambridge : Cambridge University Press, 2000 .

————— . *Structural Semantics* . Oxford : Blackwell, 2003 .

Mooij, J. A. *A Study of Metaphor* . Amsterdam : North Holland, 2005 .

Nida, E. *Componential Analysis of Meaning* . The Hague : Mouton, 2006 .

Ogden, C. K. *Opposition* . Bloomington, Ind : Indiana University Press, 2000 .

Palmer, F. R. *Semantics,* 2nd edition . Cambridge : Cambridge University Press, 2006 .

————— . *Semantics : A new Introduction* . Cambridge : University Press, 2005 .

Pulman, S. G. *Word Meaning and Belief* . London : Croom Helm, 2003 .

Putnam, H. *Realism and Reason* . Cambridge : Cambridge University Press, 2004 .

Quine, W. V. *Methods of Logic* . Cambridge, MA : Harvard University Press, 2001 .

————— . *Roots of Reference* . LaSalle : Open Court, 2000 .

————— . *Theories and Things* . Cambridge MA : Harvard University Press, 1999 .

————— . *Word and Object* . New York : Wiley, 2005 .

Russell, B. *Human Knowledge, its Scope, and its Limits* . New York : Simon & Schuster, 2006 .

Ryle, G. *The Concept of Mind* . New York : Barnes & Noble, 2001 .

Tarski, A. *Introduction to Logic* . Oxford : Oxford University Press, 2002 .

———— . *Logic, Semantics, Metamathematics* . Oxford : Clarendon, 2003 .

Vendler, Z. *Linguistics in Philosophy* . Ithaca, NY : Cornell University Press, 2004 .

Appendix I : Symbols

≠	differs from, not equal to, not synonymous with
*	ungrammatical
=	a synonym of
⊃	a hyponym of
→	entail, entailment
≡	a paraphrase of
≢	not a paraphrase of
+	existent, plus (for features)
–	non-existent, minus, not (for features)
Ø	not applicable
↔	antonymy
⊐	implies
⇒	is transformed into
&	and
v	or
~	negation (in logic)
~ ~	negation of negation
→→	is a condition of
∴	therefore

Appendix II : Abbreviations

CS	compound sentence	U	utterance
DW	deictic word	V	verb
E	expression	WA	word ambiguity
F	false		
GA	grammatical ambiguity		
L	language		
LE	language expression		
M	meaning		
M_1	sentence meaning		
M_2	speaker's meaning		
M_3	hearer's meaning		
N	noun		
NP	noun phrase		
NRE	non-referring expression		
P	proposition		
PE	predicating expression		
R	referent		
RE	referring expression		
S	sentence		
SA	sentence ambiguity		
SF	semantic field		
SM	sentence meaning		
T	true		

Subject Index

abstracts   138

additional meaning   108

affinity antonymy   71

affix   110

agent   111 , 112

ambiguity   81

ambiguity of senses   81

ambiguous words   82

analysis of meaning   118

analytical meaning   96

analytical sentences   96

analyticity   98

and-structure   89

antonymous definition   106

antonymy   62

antonymy-contradictoriness
relationship   75

association   127

audible form   118

base   110

basic meaning   107

basic features   125

basic meaning   45

bi-antonymy   72

bilateral antonymy   72

binary antonym   64

binary antonymy   63 , 64

body movements   101

commutativity   148

complementary antonymy   64

complete synonyms   45

compound structure   69

concept of correctness   16

concept of reference   25

concept of truth   16

conceptual meaning   107

contextual meaning   100

contextual replacement   46

contradiction   97

contradictories   73

contrastive analysis   140

converse antonymy   65

converseness   66

conversers' roles   101

cumulative entailment   51

cyclic antonymy   69

definite article   32

definite NP   26

definiteness   32

deictic words   36

demonstrative definition   105

descriptive definition   105 , 106

direct speech   37

directional antonymy   68

dissimilarity of senses   62

distinctive features   120

double feature   121

echoich meaning   109

emotional meaning   103

entailment   50 , 52

entailment relationship   50

entailment-hyponymy relationship53

entailment-paraphrase relationship 52

equative sentence   27

extension   38

extension of the predicate   38

extensional antonymy   67

external factors   101

extreme antonymy   64

facial feelings   101

feature redundancy   122

figurative meaning   105

formality level   109

functional definition   105

generic noun   34

generic sentence   33

genitive structure   69

goal   113

gradability   67

gradable antonymy   66 ,67

gradation   128

grammatical ambiguity   88 , 89

grammatical distribution   119

grammatical terms   33

graphemes   9

hearer's meaning   11

hierarchical antonymy   71

homonymy   82 , 85

horizontal association   135

hyponym   49

177

hyponymous definition   106

hyponymy   48 , 49 , 52

hyponymy-synonymy relationship 49

imaginary referents 35

imaginary universe 35

indefinite article   32

inference from *and*   145

instrument   112

lexemes 99

lexical ambiguity   88

lexical meaning   98 , 99

linkers 138

linking expressions 26

linking words 144

literal meaning meaning   104

location   112

logic of *and*   144

logic of *but* 150

logic of *if* 154

logic of negators   152

logic of *or* 148

logical words   144 , 152

meaning   9

meaning   109

meaning and context   100

meaning and definition   105

meaning and external factors 101

meaning and information   13

meaning and logic 144

meaning and parts of speech 110

meaning and roles   111

meaning and stereotype   106

meaning of meaning   120

measurement of meaning   127

members of the semantic field   134

morpheme   110

morphological definitions 111

morphological meaning   99

multiple antonymy 72

multiple membership   135

mutual entailment   52

mutual hyponyms 50

mutual hyponymy 50

mutual inclusion   46

nature of the semantic field   133

necessary qualities   107

negative feature   121

negative sentences   54

noun-verb function   87

of-structure   69

one-degree predicator   31

onomatopoeic words   109

or structure   90

oral form   118

ordinal definition   106

paraphrase   47

paraphrase relationship   47

part of speech   46

partial antonyms   68

partial antonymy   68

perpendicular antonymy   67

personal pronouns   26

phonetic form   118

phonetic meaning   109

physical environment   102

polysemy   82 , 83

positive feature   121

possessive form   90

potential referents   39

predicate   29

predicate degree   30 , 31

predicating expression   25

predicator   28

premodification structure   90

prepositional-phrase structure   89

proper noun   26

proposition   17

prototype   39

psychological meaning   103

rank antonymy   70

readable form   119

real antonymy   64

recipient   112

reference   18

reference and definiteness   32

referent   10 , 19

referring expression 19, 20, 26 , 33

relative meaning   102

replacement   44

reported speech   37

result   112

rule of *and* commutativity   145

rules of semantic features   126

scaled oppositeness   128

secondary features   125

secondary meaning   108

semantic components   120

semantic definitions   110

semantic features   118 , 120 , 123

semantic field   62 , 133

semantic roles   113

semantic terms   33

semantic theory   13

semantic units   109

sense   18 , 118

sense and reference   18

sense and referent   20

sense dissimilarity   62

sense similarity   62

sentence ambiguity   87

sentence ambiguity and paraphrase   90

sentence and proposition   15

sentence and utterance   14

sentence meaning   11

similarity of senses   44

situational factors   101

speaker's meaning   11

specificity   32

spoken form   9 , 118

stereotype   107

structural ambiguity   88

stylistic distribution   119

stylistic meaning   108 , 109

sub-fields   136

superordinate   49 , 72

synonymous definition   106

synonymous words   45

synonymy   44 , 52

syntactic ambiguity   88 , 89

syntactic definitions   111

syntactic meaning   99

syntactic terms   113

synthetic sentences   96

three-degree predicator   31

time   112

tone   101

transitive-intransivie function   87

transportation   133

triangle of meaning   9

truth probabilities of *and*   146

truth probabilities of negators   153

truth probabilities of *or*   149

two-degree predicator   31

types of meaning   11 , 95

types of semantic features   121

types of semantic fields   137

ungradable antonymy   64

universe of discourse   34

utterance   14

verb voice   90

word ambiguity   88

word distribution   119

word from   118

world of facts   35

world of fiction   35

written form   9 , 118

zero feature   122

zero information   13

The Author's Books

1. *The Light of Islam*
2. *The Need for Islam*
3. *Traditions of Prophet Muhammad /B1*
4. *Traditions of Prophet Muhammad /B2*
5. *The Truth about Jesus Christ*
6. *Islam and Christianity*
7. *A Dictionary of Islamic Terms: English-Arabic & Arabic-English*
8. *A Dictionary of the Holy Quran: Arabic-English*
9. *Questions and Answers about Islam*
10. *Learn Arabic by Yourself*
11. *Simplified English Grammar*
12. *A Dictionary of Education: English- Arabic*
13. *A Dictionary of Theoretical Linguistics: English-Arabic*
14. *A Dictionary of Applied Linguistics: English-Arabic*
15. *Teaching English to Arab Students*
16. *A Workbook for English Teaching Practice*
17. *Programmed TEFL Methodology*
18. *The Teacher of English*
19. *Improve Your English*
20. *A Workbook for English II*
21. *Advance Your English*
22. *The Blessing of Islam*
23. *An Introduction to Linguistics*
24. *Comparative Linguistics: English and Arabic*
25. *A Contrastive Transformational Grammar: English-Arabic*
26. *Why have they chosen Islam?*
27. *A Contrastive Transformational Grammar: Arabic and English*
28. *The Crisis of Western Civilization*
29. *A Comparison between the Four Gospels*
30. *Methods of Teaching English at the Elementary Stage*
31. *Methods of Teaching English*
32. *Teaching English as a Foreign Language*
33. *Islamic Faith*

34. *Human Rights in Islam*

35. *Penal Codes in Islam*

36. *The Pillars of Islam*

37. *Morality in Islam*

38. *The Woman in Islam*

39. *The Only Right Choice: Islam*

40. *What do you know about Islam?*

41. *The Straight Path: Islam*

42. *Legal Translation: From English into Arabic*

43. *Humanities Translation: From English into Arabic*

44. *Science Translation: From English into Arabic*

45. *General Translation: From English into Arabic*

46. *Literary Translation: From English into Arabic*

47. *Mass-Media Translation: From English into Arabic*

48. *Administration and Finance Translation: From English into Arabic*

49. *An Introduction to Semantics*

50. *English Phonetics and Phonology*

51. *English Skills One*

52. *English Skills Two*

53. *English Grammar: Morphology*

54. *General Translation 2: From Arabic into English*

68. مدخل إلى علم اللغة	55. حقيقة عيسى المسيح
69. كيف تكتب بحثاً	56. دليل الطالب في التربية العملية
70. الاختبارات التحصيلية	57. مقارنة بين الأناجيل الأربعة
71. البريق الزائف للحضارة الغربية	58. الأصوات اللغوية
72. التحريف في التوراة	59. تعليم اللغة: حالات وتعليقات
73. اليهود من كتابهم	60. الحياة مع لغتين
74. الإسلام والنصرانية: دراسة ومقارنة	61. تعلم الإملاء بنفسك
75. الاختبارات اللغوية	62. المهارات الدراسية
76. أساليب التدريس العامة	63. أساليب تدريس اللغة العربية
77. علم الدلالة (علم المعنى)	64. دراسات لغوية
78. الإسلام والحضارة الغربية	65. معجم علم الأصوات (عربي-عربي)
79. نور الإسلام (باللغة اليابانية)	66. التراكيب الشائعة في اللغة العربية
	67. قواعد تحويلية للغة العربية

183

Printed in the United States
By Bookmasters